SAA Cooperative Processing

SAA
Cooperative Processing

Mainframe to PC Connectivity

Peter Coates

Prentice Hall
New York London Toronto Sydney Tokyo Singapore

First published 1992 by
Prentice Hall International (UK) Ltd
66 Wood Lane End, Hemel Hempstead
Hertfordshire HP2 4RG
A division of
Simon & Schuster International Group

Typeset in 11/12½pt Sabon
by VAP Publishing Services, Kidlington, Oxford ˙

Printed and bound in Great Britain by
Dotesios Ltd, Trowbridge, Wiltshire.

Library of Congress Cataloging-in-Publication Data

Coates, A. P. (A. Peter)
   SAA : cooperative processing / A.P. Coates.
     p.   cm.
   Includes index.
   ISBN 0–13–787854–0
   1. IBM Systems Application Architecture. 2. Electronic digital
   computers—Programming. I. Title.
   QA76.9.A73C59 1992
   004.2′2—dc20
                                  91–20031
                                      CIP

British Library Cataloguing in Publication Data

Coates, A.P.
   SAA Cooperative processing.
   I. Title
   004.6

   ISBN 0–13–787854–0

1 2 3 4 5   96 95 94 93 92

Contents

Contents

Contents

Preface

The first cooperative processes written in any enterprise are likely be written by two people: a PC programmer and a mainframe programmer. Not only do they not have a common vocabulary to describe what they are trying to do, but each is also dealing with an unfamiliar area. They will typically start with a complete lack of appreciation of the capabilities of the machines outside their own familiar environment. Thus the PC programmer will believe that the mainframe is an expensive anachronism, and the mainframe programmer will believe the PC is only a toy and the PC programmers have just been playing and do not know what life is all about.

The purpose of this book is not only to introduce the concepts of cooperative processing and to explain in concrete detail the SAA mechanism for writing applications in such a way that both the PC and mainframe programmer will be able to understand, but also to give them an appreciation at least of how it is done in the other environment. This mutual understanding is the essence of SAA.

For further information the author can be contacted directly on 0436–78764 or +44 436 78764.

1 SAA and APPC: What and Why?

1.1 SAA APPLICATIONS

Mainframe installations come in two types: newly upgraded and overstretched. These are not mutually exclusive conditions: upgrading a mainframe is an expensive and disruptive activity. It is possible to interpret IBM's system application architecture (SAA) as a means of reducing the load on mainframes, or at least of getting more for the users from the same power.

SAA is touted as being all about the ability to move applications from one family of machines to another. Generally speaking this is really quite absurd. It makes no more sense to run a spreadsheet program on a mainframe than it does to attempt to migrate an IMS application to a PC. SAA is about moving parts of applications from one family of machines to another.

There are, however, some applications or parts of applications where it does make sense to move them from one machine to another, or to have them available on several different types of machines. Print servers and database servers are obvious examples, and it is likely that other services will be wanted from departmental and corporate computer centres and from network servers. Thus it is important that SAA standardizes not only the interfaces between computers, but also, where practical, the program environment.

Different IBM machines and operating systems have different strengths and weaknesses. Customer information control system (CICS), for instance provides an environment in which it is relatively straightforward to write transaction programs, i.e. programs that take a user request with data, process it against a database, and reply.

1

The PC, especially under OS/2, is particularly good at running programs that require fast and frequent interaction with the user, e.g. window, icon, mouse and pull-down menu (WIMP) programs. Put these two together so that the mainframe is providing a transaction-based server function for the PCs, and the interaction between the different transactions and the navigation between the different functions is all done in the PC, and you have the basis of a truly excellent system.

What is extraordinary about this type of solution is that the load on the mainframe is actually decreased as the functionality, as perceived by the user, is increased. The complexity of the mainframe programs also decreases as each transaction can now stand alone. There is a cost incurred in replacing 3270s with PS/2s, but this can be phased in with new applications, and the payback is the delaying of any need to upgrade the central processor.

The components of SAA that hold all this together are CPI-C and LU 6.2. CPI-C (Common Programming Interface-Communications) is the definition of how programs access LU 6.2. LU 6.2 is the common communications protocol provided across all IBM systems for program-to-program communications. LU 6.2, unlike the 3270 datastream for instance, is not based on the concept of a screen and a keyboard. It is designed for program-to-program use and is exceedingly efficient, and actually quite easy to use. 3270 emulation has its own special difficulties: if the mainframe program changes even trivially, then the program on the PC stops working. Systems should not be written to this interface except as a stopgap measure.

CPI-C, the SAA interface to LU 6.2, has not yet been implemented on all systems: it is, at the time of writing, only available in VM/SP release 6 and VM/ESA, although it has been announced for MVS/ESA 4.2, CICS 3.2, IMS 3.2 and the Communications Manager addon Network Services 2. However there are equivalent programming interfaces to LU 6.2 already available on CICS, AS/400s, PCs running OS/2, and to a limited extent under IMS.

The purpose of this book is to enable programmers with different technical backgrounds to understand about advanced program-to-program communication (APPC) as implemented in both their own environment and other environments. They should then be able to collaborate with each other to write cooperative systems split over different types of computer.

1.2 DESIGNING COOPERATIVE PROCESSES

When starting to design an application that involves cooperative processing and that uses machines and environments which have quite different characteristics, it is essential that you have a clear idea of the strengths and weaknesses of the machines involved. This will enable you to decide where the data are to be kept, where they are to be processed, and where the clean interfaces are.

A mainframe running CICS, for instance, is not the best place to maintain user context between functions. CICS is a transaction-based system, and although it is possible to pass information from one context to another, it is not a strong point of the system. The user context should be kept in the PC, with the user.

When considering the location of the data, clearly one wants to have a single copy of the data in the system. This makes life much simpler: maintaining consistency across multiple machines may be possible, but there is no need to make life difficult. On the other hand you do not want the programs on the PCs making unnecessary requests to the mainframe for data when they could remember some things from one transaction to the next. There is clearly a contradiction here and part of the system design involves resolving this contradiction.

1.2.1 CICS strengths

CICS provides a reasonably quick and flexible transaction-processing environment. It is good at holding very large databases, controlling access to these databases, and maintaining their consistency. To get the best out of CICS you want the transaction programs to be small, and to start, process and complete as quickly as possible. You do not want a transaction program to wait for a response from a program on the PC if that can be avoided. Still less do you want the transaction program to wait for a response from a user. Nevertheless, CICS is capable of providing much more than simply a database server facility for a set of PC programs.

1.2.2 OS/2 strengths

The new PCs and PS/2s are not toys: they are powerful computers. OS/2 is a sophisticated operating system providing a much richer environment than CICS. PCs can have a lot of memory and hundreds of megabytes of disk space. They are capable of providing much more than terminal emulation or even just a graphic user interface to a suite of CICS transactions. Programs can be large and can run continuously. They are quite different from transaction programs as found in a CICS environment. Memory and CPU requirements tend not to be a problem. PC memory is much cheaper than mainframe memory, and the PC has a processor that is typically a tenth of the power of a mainframe processor, but is dedicated to one user.

1.3 FUNCTION AND DATA DISTRIBUTION

These relative strengths lead to some fairly obvious conclusions:

1 The main data for the system must be held on the mainframe, and any processing associated with the central system, rather than the user, should be carried out there.
2 Any data held on the PC must be either transitory or not regarded as definitive or totally trustworthy: perhaps a cache of frequently accessed quasi-static data.
3 Processing done on the PC should be preliminary data-checking or perhaps the maintenance of a local log or production of local hard copy.

There is a balance to be struck over the amount of data held on the PC. The more data that is held there, the more the PC can do autonomously, but the difficulty lies in keeping it accurate and consistent with the mainframe. If little or no data is held on the PC, then the PC is reduced almost to the level of a terminal.

Consider, for instance, the example of an order entry system. Here the workstation would be expected to verify all the fields, check the customer number, etc., before starting a transaction on the mainframe to add the order to a database. The verification of a customer number consists of checking that the number is valid, checking the credit rating of the customer, and verifying the customer name is correct by asking the customer.

This last function requires that the data must be presented to the user before the main part of the transaction is run. This implies that the PC program either has to hold the customer record locally or has to ask for the data from the mainframe. You do not want the delay associated in running an additional transaction on the mainframe if it can be avoided, but the PC cannot hold your entire customer file. However the customer descriptions are typically reasonably static, and typically only a few customers account for the bulk of the orders. Thus if the PC maintains a cache of a 100 or so customer records and only asks the mainframe for customer details when it does not know then you would have the best of both worlds. Clearly, the main transaction program would reject an order if the customer record were out of date, and that action would cause the customer record on the PC to be updated or deleted.

The contents of the customer detail cache, or any similar data set held on the PC, can be standardized over the entire system, or can be allowed to be specific to each workstation. Which is best depends on whether each workstation tends to perform the same functions, or whether there is a degree of specialization, formalized or just by usage. If the data held on each workstation is to be standardized you need to consider how these data are to be distributed and maintained, which brings us on to the subject of start-of-session processing.

1.4 START-OF-SESSION PROCESSING

When the part of the system that runs on a PC is started by a user, it is important for all sorts of reasons that it starts a start-of-session transaction on the host. In this way revised data and even revised programs can be sent to the PC: this can be vital. No matter how well designed a system is, you cannot rule out the possibility that at some point in the future the protocol defined between the programs will change. Nor can you be absolutely confident that some user is not using an old version of the software. If the start-of-session includes the PC sending version numbers or dates to the mainframe, then the mainframe can reply by sending new versions of programs or data files. This could result in a massive surge in network traffic at 9.00 on the

Monday morning after a program change, the sort of surge that could bring a network to its knees. Clearly for large systems a more sophisticated system would be needed.

One such approach would be to keep a register at the host of all client machines that run certain programs. The mainframe could then send out updates in the middle of the night to those machines. However, this approach too has its difficulties. First, the tables on the host would have to be maintained, a non-trivial activity. Second, all the client machines would have to be left switched on and receptive at all times, which is not necessarily the normal working practice for PCs.

A third solution is a mixture of the two: the central computer could keep a list of outlying computers that were responsible for maintaining up-to-date copies of all software. When a program change was made the mainframe could then distribute the updates to these outlying computers (typically PS/2s). When the users started work in the morning, their initial conversations would be with these local computers, so that any peak traffic could be restricted to the local LAN. The same method could be used to distribute any data that are held by the workstations.

There are a number of packages available today that perform this necessary task. One such is IBM's NetView/ DM, which maintains a central copy of programs and data that may be distributed to outlying sites via a 'plan' containing filenames, remote site names, etc.

1.5 TRANSACTION PROGRAM AND PROTOCOL DESIGN

Each CICS transaction program should be written to perform one function. This could be something like taking an order, verifying all the fields, checking the customer number, etc. and adding the order to a database. All the complexity involved in passing context from one transaction program to another should be quite irrelevant. If you find yourself in the position where context is being held on the mainframe you should look very hard at the division of the system between the PC and the CICS.

When a workstation is sending data to a mainframe transaction program, it ought to wait for a reply indicating successful completion: either a confirmation response or reply data. Otherwise the operator does not know whether the transaction was successful. On the other hand, when the mainframe sends data to the PC, it is usually less critical that the mainframe be aware of whether the PC has processed them successfully, especially as processing in this context is likely to mean displaying. Also, in general, when the PC is sending data to the mainframe the operator is willing to wait for a response. It makes less sense for a mainframe transaction to be held for a confirmation response when none is really needed.

1.6 INTRODUCTION TO SYSTEM NETWORK ARCHITECTURE (SNA)

Before you can really appreciate how to use APPC to communicate between programs, and especially before you can configure a PC and a mainframe so that they can communicate, it is important to have some idea of the underlying concepts of SNA. These are the PU, the LU, the session and the conversation.

An SNA network is a network of computers. In SNA parlance a computer is a **physical unit** (PU). The word 'computer' here is being used in a broad sense, meaning not only central processors such as 3090s, but also front-end processors such as 3745s, and terminal controllers such as 3174s. PUs are connected by real connections called **Lines**. A PU is something you can touch. A **logical unit** (LU) is a less obvious construct (see Fig. 1.1).

Figure 1.1 A line connects two PUs

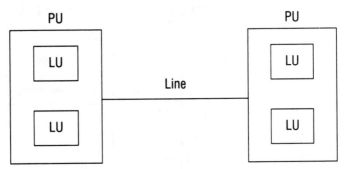

Rarely do we want computers themselves to communicate. More typically, we want a terminal to communicate with an application. Terminals and applications are examples of SNA LUs. Terminals seem particularly solid examples of LUs, but in fact one physical terminal may well be several logical terminals, each of which will be an LU.

Within the central processor (which will be a PU), there may be several invocations of CICS running. Each of these will be an LU. When a terminal logs on to CICS, it is establishing an SNA connection called a **session** between two LUs, the terminal and CICS.

For terminals, there is typically only one session per LU–LU pair. When you establish a connection between two instances of CICS, you may want a group of equivalent sessions so that several transaction programs can communicate at once. This is done by establishing a **session group** of parallel sessions.

Within CICS there will be some **transaction programs** (TPs). When a terminal accesses a transaction program it has a **conversation** with it. Only one conversation at a time may use a session.

Summary

There are physical units (PUs), which are connected by lines and which control logical units (LUs). LUs are connected by sessions and may control transaction programs (TPs). Sessions carry conversations which run either between an LU and a TP or between TPs (see Fig. 1.2).

Figure 1.2 Sessions connect LUs: conversations connect TPs

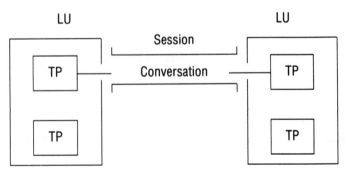

1.7 INTRODUCTION TO LU TYPE 6.2

An LU type 6.2 session is one type of connection defined within SNA. LU 6.2 is designed for communication between two programs, unlike LU 2 which is the standard LU for communication between a terminal and a transaction program.

With programmable workstations, the workstation itself is a PU, and may contain several LUs. The SNA network is defined so that there is a line between that PU and the mainframe PU, and sessions between the LUs in the workstation and the LUs, such as CICS, in the mainframe. Programs in the workstation can then use these LUs to establish conversations with transaction programs in the LUs in the mainframe, e.g. CICS transactions.

The LU 6.2 protocol that these conversations use is not unlike that used in radio telephony:

- You have to establish the connection, which in LU 6.2 terms is done by issuing an ALLOCATE.
- It is up to the person who is talking to turn the line around by saying 'Over', or in LU 6.2 terms by issuing a PREPARE_TO_RECEIVE.
- It is possible to interrupt, but data is likely to be lost. It is in the area of these interruptions and the confirmation of receipt ('Did you get that? Over') that most of APPC's apparent complexity arises.

There is one additional point that has to be borne in mind when programming using APPC that is different from radio telephony. APPC communication is buffered, and is essentially a lazy mechanism. APPC will not send anything to the partner TP until it absolutely has to. For instance, if you send some data and then listen for a reply, APPC will not send the data until after you issue the call to turn the line around. This makes for efficient communications, but rather confuses the issue of return codes: initially it seems strange that you can have an allocation failure (notification that no conversation was started) on a receive when you have apparently successfully sent data.

1.7.1 APPC and Netbios

There is some obvious overlap in functionality between APPC and Netbios. However, Netbios is limited in that it is only supported by DOS and OS/2 on PCs and not at all on other IBM computers, and cannot operate across SNA networks. Netbios is appropriate for use between PCs running DOS as the implementation of APPC takes up too much memory to be reasonable.

REFERENCE FOR SNA INTRODUCTION   *System Network Architecture Technical Overview*, IBM Corporation, Mechanicsburgh, PA, 17 March 1983.

2 Programming for APPC

APPC has a quite undeserved reputation for being difficult. It is in fact about as simple as it can be and yet still provide the required functions. Basically, only one program can talk at a time in any given conversation, and it is up to the program speaking to change the direction of the conversation.

The most complicated part of APPC is the number of things you can do when you have control of the conversation, that is when you are in **send** state, and symmetrically, the number of things that can happen when you are in **receive** state.

In send state you can do any of the following:

- Send data.
- Hand control over to the other side.
- Request confirmation that the data sent so far are acceptable.
- Terminate the conversation.
- Request confirmation and turn the conversation around.
- Request a final confirmation before terminating the conversation.
- Send an error indication.

In receive state you can receive any of the following:

- Data.
- Notification that you now control the conversation and can send.
- A request for confirmation of data to date.
- Notification that the conversation has been terminated.
- A request for you to confirm data to date and notification that the conversation has been turned round.

11

- A confirm-and-terminate request.
- Notification of an error.

In some implementations of APPC you receive data with status information. For instance, if the sender sends data followed by a request for confirmation, then the receiver will, in certain implementations, receive both at the same time.

It is also possible in some implementations to send in one action both data and the control information that logically follows it. This is not necessarily good practice.

It is the various forms of control information that cause APPC to have several more states than just send and receive. These will be dealt with later. But before that we have a description of a minimal subset of APPC. This is sufficient for simple programs to talk together, but it does not contain the features designed for reporting success or failure to the partner program.

Before even the minimal subset is described, there has to be a description of the mechanism for invoking the APPC functions. We are interested in several different environments on several different types of computer, and inevitably the invoking mechanisms differ. The machines and environments covered by this book are as follows:

- OS/2 Extended Edition on a PC or PS/2.
- CICS under DOS/VSE or MVS on a 370 family computer.
- CPI-C implemented on VM/CMS.
- OS/400 on the AS/400.
- IMS on a 370 family computer.

IMS is a rather special case, in that until IMS/ESA V3.2 there is no APPC interface *per se*, but there is a limited bridge that enables APPC programs to interface with IMS transactions. IMS is therefore dealt with separately. The other four environments are all dealt with together, and each APPC function is described in terms of all four systems. This approach should help to clarify the interface in an unfamiliar environment by having it described along side the more familiar one(s).

APPC is also supported by several other manufacturers on a wide range of machines, such as the Apple Macintosh and DEC VAX. There are also several other implementations of APPC available for the PC both under OS/2 and DOS, such as the DCA Select Communications products. The DCA Select Communications Server deserves particular attention in that it provides a mechanism whereby DOS workstations can use APPC without a huge memory overhead. The program interface offered by third-party APPC products is usually the same as the IBM API.

2.2 A PAIR OF APPC PROGRAMS

Before a pair of programs on two different computers can communicate they have first to make contact. With APPC this is done by having the originating program issue an `Allocate` naming the program it wants to talk to. This causes the named program to be started at the far end. A typical pair of programs might be a program on a PC wanting to retrieve information from a program on a mainframe system. Ignoring any possible error conditions for the present, the two programs will have the form of Fig. 2.1.

Figure 2.1 A pair of APPC programs

PC side (originating)   **CICS side (destination)**

```
ALLOCATE specifying local ──────▶ (TP started by CICS)
LU, partner LU, Mode, and
remote TP Name
Send_data request         ──────▶ Receive_and_wait
                                      request with change
                                      direction indication

Prepare_to_receive
Receive_and_wait          ◀────── Send_data reply with end of
      data=reply                          conversation indicator
Receive_and_wait          ◀────── end
      ret=deallocate
end
```

The verbs used in Fig. 2.1 are as follows:

`Allocate`	Sets up the conversation, specifying the resources to be used

	and the name of the program to be run at the far end.
`Send_data`	Sends data, and in some environments extra information such as change of direction or end of conversation.
`Prepare_to_receive`	Is necessary in some environments to change the direction of the conversation.
`Receive_and_wait`	Receives data or status information such as change of direction or end of conversation.

The actual form of these APPC verbs in the various environments and the possible return codes are described in the rest of this chapter. At the end of the chapter there are several examples showing typical interactions between programs on PCs and in the various different environments. However, before the various functions are considered, it makes sense to look at how they are accessed.

2.2.1 Accessing the APPC functions

OS/2

On the PC under OS/2, the APPC functions are referred to as verbs. To issue one of the APPC verbs you have to pass a control block to the APPC entry point.

```
# include <appc_c.h>

unsigned char tp_id[8];
unsigned long conv_id;

//issue MC_PREPARE_TO_RECEIVE for TP_id, conv_id
struct prepare_to_receive prepare_to_receive_cb;

// set verb operation code and extension
prepare_to_receive_cb.opcode = AP_M_PREPARE_TO_RECEIVE;
prepare_to_receive_cb.opext = AP_MAPPED_CONVERSATION;
prepare_to_receive_cb.reserv2 = 0;        /* Reserved */

memcpy(prepare_to_receive_cb.tp_id, tp_id,sizeof(tp_id));
prepare_to_receive_cb.conv_id = conv_id;
prepare_to_receive_cb.ptr_type = AP_FLUSH;
```

```
prepare_to_receive_cb.locks = AP_SHORT;

APPC_C((long)&prepare_to_receive_cb);
// the return code is prepare_to_receive_cb.primary_rc
// more error status in
     prepare_to_receive_cb.secondary_rc
```

The OS/2 examples use a C callable library which is included in Appendix B. The library routines call APPC_C.

CICS

Under CICS, the APPC functions are accessed from COBOL or Assembler by using the EXEC-CICS interface and issuing CICS commands such as:

```
EXEC CICS RECEIVE INTO(buffer) LENGTH(length)
                                END—EXEC
```

Many of the CICS APPC commands, like the one just given, are very similar to the ones used for communicating with 3270 terminals.

CPI-C

In CPI-C the interface is through a set of callable functions. There are three types of function: those that set local parameters which affect the action of the other verbs; those that extract returned information; and those that actually do something. The last functions are the same as those provided by APPC under CICS or under OS/2. Thus, for example, a receive verb in CPI-C would look like

```
[CALL "CMSF" USING conversation—ID,
                    Set_Fill,
                    return—code.]
* optionally set the fill type for basic
* conversations
  [CALL "CMSRT" USING conversation—ID,
                      Set_Receive_Type,
                      return—code.]
* optionally set receive type
  CALL "CMRCV" USING conversation_ID,
```

```
buffer,
requested_length,
data_received,
received_length,
status_received,
request_to_send_received,
return_code.
```

AS/400

On the AS/400, the interface to APPC is by means of the standard READ and WRITE statements in RPG or COBOL. The file used for a conversation is called an ICF file, and is mapped on to a particular destination by using the OVRICFDEVE or ADDICFDEVE command at the main command level:

```
OVRICFDEVE PGMDEV(pgmdevname) RMTLOCNAME(location)
```

'Pgmdevname' is the name by which the ICF file is known to the program, 'location' is the name given to an entry in the remote location list. For a program that is to be started remotely, instead of specifying a location for RMTLOCNAME, specify *REQUESTER. See Chapter 5 for information about setting up remote location lists.

The control functions such as prepare-to-receive are achieved by means of keywords in the format specifications for the I/O statement. These format statements can be either system-supplied formats such as $$SEND to send data and invite a reply, i.e. send and prepare-to-receive, or user defined in DDS definition for the ICF file such as:

```
A          R SNDINV
A    45                          INVITE
```

These would be used in a COBOL program as follows:

```
01   INV-REC-O.
     03   REC-LEN       PIC 9(4) VALUE IS 0.

PREPARE-TO-RECEIVE.
     WRITE ICFREC FROM INV-REC-O FORMAT IS "$$SEND"
```

or, using a user-defined format:

```
01    INV-REC-O.
      03 REC-LEN        PIC 9(4) VALUE IS O.


PREPARE-TO-RECEIVE.
    MOVE INDON TO CMNF-INDIC(45).
    WRITE ICFREC FROM INV-REC-O FORMAT IS "SNDINV"
        INDICATORS ARE CMNF-INDIC-AREA.
```

Using user-defined formats has a distinct advantage when it comes to receiving conversation status. A program either can determine whether a conversation turnaround has been received in the return code from the read, or, if using a user-defined format, can arrange for an indicator to be set when one is received. This is done by specifying the indicator in the format in the DDS source:

```
A        R RCVTRND
A                          RCVTRNRND(40 'END OF TRN')
```

The ICF file then needs to be created. This is done using the CRTICFF command:

```
CRTICFF  FILE(filename)
        SRCFILE(source-filename)
        SRCMBR(member-name)
        ACQPGMDEV(pgmdevname)
        TEXT('comment')
```

2.3 THE ESSENTIAL SUBSET

The essential subset is that which enables a program to establish a conversation with another, to exchange data, and to terminate the conversation. The functions are as follows:

- To initiate a conversation.
- To accept an incoming conversation.
- To send data.
- To change the direction of the conversation.
- To receive data.
- To terminate a conversation.

2.3.1 *Starting a conversation*

Starting a conversation is one of the less architected areas of APPC. This is because it interacts with highly system-dependent functions such as how programs are started, and what programs are. A conversation is defined as communication between two transaction programs. Any program running in CICS is a transaction program, but to be a transaction program on the PC, a program has to register with the communications manager first. This is done by issuing the verb TP_STARTED. In CPI-C and on the AS/400 the concept of an originating TP is not present. The local LU is considered to be part of the conversation parameters.

In the formal model of APPC, the issuing of an ALLOCATE verb causes the specified transaction program to be started on the remote LU. What actually happens may be slightly different. This is discussed in more detail in Chapter 4.

The name of the transaction program specified in the ALLOCATE varies from system to system.

OS/2   A transaction program name in the incoming allocate is a string of up to 64 characters starting with an upper-case letter and containing only letters and numbers. The characters $, # and @ are considered to be letters.

CICS   A transaction program name in the incoming allocate can only be 4 characters long, but names up to 32 characters long can be specified in the allocate command.

CPI-C   A transaction program in the incoming allocate can be up to 8 characters long, but names up to 64 characters long can be specified in the allocate command.

AS/400   A transaction program name consists of two parts, the program name and the library. For incoming allocates these are separated by a '.', with the program name coming first. The two names can each be up to 10 characters long. If the program is in a default library, then the library name need not be specified. Valid TP names look like PGM, or PGM.LIB. When issuing an allocate from an AS/400, the program name is specified in a special way. See the description under AS/400 below.

OS/2

The TP_STARTED verb takes two parameters: the alias of the local LU under which the TP is deemed to be running, and the name of the TP. Remember that CICS is an LU, and that all TPs have names and run under CICS. The communications manager, in this respect, has delusions of grandeur and likes to think of itself as being in control of programs, rather than being used by them. At least the terminology works that way.

If the TP_STARTED verb succeeds, it returns a TP identifier (id). This TP_id has to be passed to all subsequent APPC calls for this transaction program.

To start a conversation with a remote transaction program the local transaction program issues the verb MC_ALLOCATE. This starts the remote transaction program, and sets up a conversation between the two programs.

On the PC, the parameters that are passed to MC_ALLOCATE are the TP_id, the alias of the remote LU, the mode name, the name of the remote TP, the conversation type, the sync_level and the security parameters. For the moment we are only interested in what are called **mapped conversations**. The other conversation type is **basic**, which offers little advantage and is not supported by COBOL under CICS. For our essential subset we only need sync_level = AP_FLUSH. We will look at the other sync_levels later. Security does not affect us at this point either.

If the allocate succeeds, it returns a conversation id which, along with the TP_id, has to be passed to all verbs concerning this conversation:

```
char     lu_alias[9] = "local lu alias";
#define TP_NAME_LEN     8
char     tp_name[TN_NAME_LEN];
char     tp_id[8];
char     partner_lu_alias[9] = "remote lu alias";
char     mode_name[8];
#define TPN_LEN 8
char     tpn[TPN_LEN];
long     conv_id;
long     ret2;
```

```
convert(SV_ASCII_TO_EBCDIC, SV_AE, TP_NAME_LEN,
                "local TP name", tp_name);
convert(SV_ASCII_TO_EBCDIC, SV_AE, TPN_LEN,
                "partner TP name", tpn);
if (APPC_tp_started(lu_name, tp_name, tp_name_len, tp_id))
    return -1;
ret = APPC_MC_allocate(tp_id,
                partner_lu_name, mode_name,
                tpn, tpn_len,
                AP_WHEN_SESSION_ALLOCATED,
                AP_FLUSH, // sync level
                AP_NONE,  // security type
                NULL, 0,  // user id & user id length
                NULL, 0,  // password & length
                &conv_id,
                &ret2);
```

These calls, as in all the PC examples that follow, use the subroutines listed in Appendix B.

CICS

Under CICS, starting a conversation is also a two-part process, but is quite different from how it is done on the PC. You start by issuing the following:

```
EXEC CICS ALLOCATE  SYSID(name)
                    [PROFILE(name)]
                    [NOQUEUE]
                                        END-EXEC
```

Where SYSID is the SYSIDENT from the Terminal Control Table (TCT) entry representing the remote LU which is on the PC, PROFILE you typically will want to allow to default: it specifies the class of service (priority) assigned to the session allocated for the conversation. NOQUEUE tells CICS not to wait until a session is available, but to succeed or fail straight away. This call gives the program ownership of the session with the remote LU. A handle for this resource is returned in the Exec Interface Block (EIB) variable EIBRSRCE. This handle will be the conversation id once the conversation has been fully established. This is done by issuing the following:

```
EXEC CICS CONNECT   PROCESS CONVID(conv-id)
                    PROCNAME(name)
                    PROCLENGTH(name)
                    SYNCLEVEL(0 ¦ 1 ¦ 2)
                    [PIPLIST(name)
                    PIPLENGTH(name)]
                                        END-EXEC
```

where `conv-id` is the resource handle returned from the `ALLOCATE`, and `PROCNAME` and `PROCLENGTH` give the name of the remote TP to be started. For our essential subset `SYNCLEVEL` should be 0, which is the same as specifying AP_FLUSH on the PC. There is usually no point in a CICS process providing PIP (Program Initialization Parameter) data for a TP, as neither the communications manager on the PC nor CPI-C have any way of receiving it, although the AS/400 does.

CPI-C

Under CPI-C, instead of the program having to specify the local and remote LU names, the mode name and the remote TP name, you only have to specify a **symbolic destination name**. This name is looked up in the **side information table** which contains all the characteristics and names needed to allocate a conversation. Thus allocating a conversation with a remote TP involves two active calls, `CMINIT` to extract the default TP and communications parameters for the TP from the side information, and `CMALLC` to initiate the conversation. Between the two calls there may be several parameter-setting calls to override the defaults. An example is shown below:

```
MOVE "sym-dest-name" TO SYM-DEST-NAME.
CALL "CMINIT" USING Conversation-id
                    Sym-dest-name
                    Return-code.
* optionally followed by calls to change all the
* parameter values picked up from sym-dest-name
* from the side information
  CALL "CMALLC" USING Conversation-id
                    Return-code.
```

AS/400

To allocate a conversation from an AS/400 program you need to do several things. First, you must open the ICF file, which automatically acquires the program device if the ACQPGMDEV parameter is specified on the CRTICFF command. Otherwise you have to acquire the device.

Then the program has to issue an EVOKE command. This, like most APPC commands, is done by writing to the program using a format that specifies the keyword EVOKE. There is a system-provided format for allocating conversations: $$EVOKNI. Do not specify a library name in the evoke if the destination is not an AS/400.

In the DDS source:

```
    R EVOKPGM
A 50                        EVOKE(&PGMID)
A    PGMID     10A P
```

In the COBOL program:

```
01  ICFREC.
    COPY DDS-ALL-FORMATS OF SRCICF.

    OPEN I-O SRCICF.

    MOVE "tp-name" TO PGMID OF EVOKPGM-O.
    MOVE INDON TO CMNF-INDIC(50).
    WRITE ICFREC FORMAT IS "EVOKPGM"
        INDICATORS ARE CMNF-INDIC-AREA.

    MOVE INOFF TO CMNF-INDIC(50).
```

2.3.2 Accepting an incoming conversation

The initial behaviour of a program designed to accept an incoming allocate varies enormously from system to system. Under CICS, on the AS/400 and on the PC for 'non-queued attach manager started' programs, the program is started automatically when the allocate arrives. Private resources can be started by AVS (APPC/VM VTAM Support) in the same way. For global resources accessed through AVS and 'queued operator started' programs on the PC, the target programs have to be running before the allocates arrive in order to receive them. The various ways in which the systems can be set up, and the effect this has on the programs, are discussed in Chapter 4.

OS/2

A program on the PC is typically started by the communications manager, but even then it must issue a verb to receive the incoming allocate. This is done by issuing the verb RECEIVE_ALLOCATE and specifying the name of the transaction program. This verb, if it succeeds, returns the following information:

- The TP_id for the transaction program.
- The conversation_id for the conversation.
- The sync_level, which for the essential subset is NONE.
- The conversation_type, which for the essential subset is mapped.
- The user name, if security was specified.
- The alias of the local LU being used.
- The alias of the partner LU.
- The mode name for the session.

The TP id and the conversation id are needed for all subsequent verbs issued in this conversation. An example of a call to RECEIVE_ALLOCATE is shown below:

```
convert (SV_ASCII_TO_EBCDIC, SV_AE, 64,
          "local TP name filled with spaces",
          tp_name);
ret = APPC_receive_allocate(tp_name,
              tp_id,
              &conv_id,
              &sync_level,
              &conversation_type,
              user_id,
              lu_alias,
              partner_lu_alias,
              mode_name,
              &ret2);
```

CICS

A CICS transaction program does not need to do anything to accept an incoming conversation. If it wants to, it can obtain details about the conversation by issuing an EXEC CICS EXTRACT PROCESS call, but the conversation is the **principal facility** and so does not need to be specified on subsequent CICS commands for that conversation.

CPI-C

For global resources accessed through a global AVS gateway, there must be a program already running in a CMS machine which has identified itself as a resource manager for the resource. This is done by using the XCIDRM function. It can then wait for an event to take place for that resource by issuing the XCWOE call. If the event is XC-ALLOCATION-REQUEST then the CPI-C program must issue the call CMACCP to accept the incoming allocate. This returns a conversation-ID, and a return-code. It also sets the conversation characteristics, which can be examined using the appropriate extract calls. This is discussed in more detail in Chapter 4.

```
* IDENTIFY OURSELVES TO VM AS A GLOBAL RESOURCE
      MOVE 'resource-name' TO RESOURCE-ID.
      MOVE 2 TO RESOURCE-MANAGER-TYPE.
      MOVE 0 TO SERVICE-MODE.
      MOVE 1 TO SECURITY-LEVEL-FLAG.
      CALL 'XCIDRM' USING RESOURCE-ID
                          RESOURCE-MANAGER-TYPE
                          SERVICE-MODE
                          SECURITY-LEVEL-FLAG
                          CM-RETCODE.
      CALL 'XCWOE' USING RESOURCE-ID
                          CONVERSATION-ID
                          EVENT-TYPE
                          DATA-LENGTH
                          CONSOLE-INPUT-BUFFER
                          CM-RETCODE.
      IF  CM-OK
          NEXT SENTENCE
      ELSE
```

```
            DISPLAY 'ERROR WITH WAIT-ON-EVENT',
                     CM-RETCODE
            GO TO END-PROGRAM
      IF  XC-ALLOCATION-REQUEST
            NEXT SENTENCE
      ELSE
            DISPLAY 'UNKNOWN WAIT ON EVENT TYPE',
                     EVENT_TYPE
            GO TO END-PROGRAM.
      CALL 'CMACCP' USING CONVERSATION-ID
                            CM-RETCODE.
      IF  CM-OK
            DISPLAY 'CONVERSATION ALLOCATED'
      ELSE
            DISPLAY 'UNABLE TO ALLOCATE CONVERSATION'.
```

AS/400

To accept an incoming conversation on an AS/400 program you need to open an ICF file which has been mapped to the destination *REQUESTER. If you specified the ACQPGMDEV parameter on the CRTICFF command, then the program device is automatically acquired. Otherwise you then have to acquire the device. The acquire, whether implicit or explicit, returns when an allocate has been accepted.

2.3.3 Sending data

Data can only be sent if the conversation is in send state for your side. Initially the TP that started the conversation is in send state.

OS/2

To send data from the PC, you issue the verb MC_SEND_DATA. The parameters passed to MC_SEND_DATA, besides the TP_id and conv_id are a pointer to the data to be sent and the length of the data. The data must be in a shared segment which can be obtained by issuing the call DosAllocSeg with ShareInd = 1. The manipulation of shared segments is done in the APPC_MC_send_data subroutine in this example: for efficiency you may want to eliminate the copying of data this implies.

```
ret = APPC_MC_send_data(tp_id, conv_id,
                        record_length,
                        (char *)&record,
                        &rts, &lret);
```

CICS

To send data from CICS, you issue the following EXEC:

```
EXEC CICS SEND [CONVID(conv-id)]
               FROM(data) LENGTH(length)
                                    END-EXEC
```

The conversation id would not need to be specified if this conversation were the principal facility, as would be the case if this conversation were started by an incoming allocate.

CPI-C

To send data using CPI-C, you call the function CMSEND. You can allow the various characteristics that affect the operation of this verb to default as the default values are correct for this subset. The function CMSEND takes the parameters conversation-ID, buffer and buffer length, and returns the parameters request-to-send-received and return-code. In a conversation using only the subset calls, request-to-send-received will not be set. This applies to all functions that return this value. Return code can only return CM_OK, or a value indicating either a programming error, a configuration error or a resource failure. The only return code that can be generated because of the behaviour of the remote program using this subset is CM_DEALLOCATED_ABEND, indicating that the partner program abended, or at least abended the conversation.

```
CALL 'CMSEND' USING CONVERSATION-ID
                    BUF
                    BUF-LEN
                    REQUEST-TO-SEND-RECEIVED
                    CM-RETCODE.
```

AS/400

To send data from an AS/400 program you simply write it to the ICF file using a suitable format. In this case you want a format that does not have any control keywords in it. The system supplied format for a simple send is $$SENDNI.

In the DDS source:

```
R SNDDATA
   SNDFLD          80A
```

In the COBOL program:

```
WRITE ICFREC FROM DATA-REC FORMAT IS "SNDDATA"
   INDICATORS ARE CMNF-INDIC-AREA.
```

In all cases you have to remember that LU 6.2 is a lazy architecture, and no data will actually be sent until either APPC runs out of buffer space or the conversation changes direction.

2.3.4 Changing the direction of a conversation

Only the TP that can currently send can change the direction of a conversation. The receiving program is very much controlled by the actions of the program currently in send state.

OS/2

On the PC the conversation is turned around by issuing the verb MC_PREPARE_TO_RECEIVE. Besides the inevitable TP_id and conv_id parameters, this verb takes two other parameters: type, which is ignored for conversations started in the way suggested for this subset, and locks, which is also ignored. This verb should not be confused with the verb MC_REQUEST_TO_SEND which does not turn the conversation around, is not in this subset, and is rarely needed.

```
ret = APPC_MC_prepare_to_receive(tp_id, conv_id,
                        AP_SYNC_LEVEL,
                        AP_SHORT);
```

CICS

On CICS the conversation is turned around by issuing the following:

```
EXEC CICS SEND [CONVID(conv-id)]
               INVITE WAIT
                                       END-EXEC
```

This can be combined with sending data, should you really want to, by issuing the command

```
EXEC CICS SEND [CONVID(conv-id)]
               FROM(data) LENGTH(length)
               INVITE WAIT
                                       END-EXEC
```

CPI-C

Using CPI-C, the function to call to turn the conversation around is CMPTR. The only settable characteristic that can affect the operation of this verb is prepare-to-receive-type, which does not affect conversations set up using the default conversation characteristics:

```
CALL 'CMPTR' USING CONVERSATION-ID
                   CM-RETCODE.
```

AS/400

For an AS/400 program to change the direction of a conversation it has to issue an INVITE command. This, like most APPC commands, is done by writing to the program using a format that specifies the keyword INVITE. The system-provided format $$SEND provides the invite function.

In the DDS source:

```
     R INVITE
A 45                              INVITE
```

In the COBOL program:

```
MOVE INDON TO CMNF-INDIC(45).
WRITE ICFREC FORMAT IS "INVITE"
    INDICATORS ARE CMNF-INDIC-AREA.
MOVE INOFF TO CMNF-INDIC(45).
```

In all environments the conversation turnaround is implied if the TP issues a receive when in send state.

2.3.5 Receiving data

Curiously, receiving is the most complicated part of the APPC interface. The reason for this is that the receive verbs return both data and status information. For instance, if the remote TP issues an MC_PREPARE_TO_RECEIVE, or an EXEC CICS SEND INVITE WAIT, then the receive verb will return an indication that the conversation is now in send state. The behaviour is also different on the PC from that under CICS or using CPI-C or APPC on the AS/400. The APPC verb MC_RECEIVE_AND_WAIT, which is the main receive verb of APPC on the PC, returns either data or status. The CICS RECEIVE command, the CPI-C CMRCV function and the AS/400 READ return all the information they can, which may be both data and status.

OS/2

On the PC, the verb MC_RECEIVE_AND_WAIT takes the inevitable TP_id and conv_id as parameters as well as the address and length of a buffer in a shared segment:

```
ret = APPC_MC_receive_and_wait(tp_id, conv_id,
                buffer, sizeof(buffer),
                &reclen, &what, &rts, &lret);
```

MC_RECEIVE_AND_WAIT returns several return values:

received data length   Is the number of bytes of data actually received.

what-received	Describes what was received by this call. This can be either data or some sort of status indicator.
request-to-send received	Is not used in this subset.
secondary return code	Is a 32-bit value that elaborates on the main return code.

The return code can take the following values in addition to various other values all of which imply programming, communications or configuration errors:

AP_OK	Either data or status were received, but not both.
AP_DEALLOC_NORMAL	The conversation was terminated by the partner program.
AP_DEALLOC_ABEND	The partner program abended, or at least abended the conversation.
Other	Implies a program or configuration error or a communications failure.

If the return code is AP_OK then what-received is also set:

AP_DATA_COMPLETE	A complete message, or the last section of one already partially received is now in the buffer. Received-length gives the length of the data received by this call.
AP_DATA_INCOMPLETE	A partial message was received. This happens when the message sent exceeds the size of the buffer passed to receive-and-wait. No data is lost, just keep reissuing receive-and-wait until you have received the whole of the message.
AP_SEND	Indicates that the partner program is now ready to receive. The local program is now in control of the conversation and can send.

MC_RECEIVE_AND_WAIT is the only verb in this subset that can legitimately be issued if the conversation is in receive state. You must issue this verb even if you know that you are going to receive a SEND indication.

CICS

Under CICS, the command to issue is

```
EXEC CICS RECEIVE [CONVID(conv-id)]
                  INTO(buffer)
                  LENGTH(length)
                  [NOTRUNCATE]
                                          END-EXEC
```

where CONVID can be omitted if you are receiving from the principal facility, i.e. the TP was started by an incoming allocate. To determine what was received you have to look at the exec interface block:

EIBNODAT Is set if no data was received, only status information.

EIBCOMPL Is set if the data received is complete. This field should only be checked if NOTRUNCATE was specified. If the buffer was too small for the data and NOTRUNCATE was not specified then the LENERR condition is raised.

EIBFREE Is set if the conversation has been terminated. After processing the data (if any), the program should free the resource by issuing a FREE command.

EIBRECV Is not zero if the conversation is still in receive state, i.e. an MC_PREPARE _TO_RECEIVE has not been issued by the remote TP.

If the remote TP abended, or abended the conversation, then the condition TERMERR is raised, EIBERR is set, and EIBERRCD is set to X'08640000'.

CPI-C

Using CPI-C, the function call to make to receive is CMRCV:

```
CALL "CMRCV" USING conversation-ID
                   buffer
                   requested-length
                   data-received
                   received-length
                   status-received
                   request-to-send-received
                   return-code.
```

where `conversation-ID` identifies the conversation, `buffer` is where any data returned is to be placed, `requested-length` is the maximum amount of data to return, `received-length` is the length of data returned, if there is any. `Request_to_send_received` is not used in this subset. `Data-received`, `status-received` and `return-code` between them indicate the result of the call. The possibilities for `return-code` are as follows:

CM–OK	Data or status or both were received.
CM–DEALLOCATED–NORMAL	The conversation was terminated by the partner program. Data but not status may also be returned.
CM–DEALLOCATED–ABEND	The partner program abended or abended the conversation.
Other	Implies a program, configuration or communication failure

If the `return-code` is CM-OK, then `data-received` and `status-received` will be set. `Data-received` will also be set when the `return-code` is CM-DEALLOCATE-NORMAL. `Data-received` can return the following values:

`CM-NO-DATA-RECEIVED`	No data was received, only status.
`CM-COMPLETE-DATA-RECEIVED`	A complete message, or the last section of one already partially received is now in the buffer. `Received-length` gives the length of the data received by this call.
`CM-INCOMPLETE-DATA-RECEIVED`	A partial message was received. This happens when the message sent exceeds the size of the buffer passed to CMRCV. No data is lost, just keep reissuing CMRCV until you have received the whole of the message.

`Status-received` can return the following values:

`CM-NO-STATUS-RECEIVED`	No status was received, only data.
`CM-SEND-RECEIVED`	Indicates that the partner program is now ready to receive. The local program is now in control of the conversation and can send.

If data is received at the same time as status, then the data logically precedes the status.

AS/400

On the AS/400 a program receives data by reading from the ICF file. The return code from the read indicates whether the read succeeded or failed, and what was received. In addition it is possible to associate indicators with the various possible status events that can be received as follows:

RCVDETACH(ind—num 'comment')   If this keyword is included in the DDS source for the ICF file then indicator ind—num will be set if the conversation was terminated by the partner program.

RCVTRNRND(ind—num 'comment')   Indicator ind—num will be set if the partner program is now ready to receive. The program with this indication is now in control of the conversation and can send.

    This information and more is also available from the return code:

major—code = 00   Data was received.

major—code = 03   No data was received.

major—code = 02   Data was received but the program is being cancelled (controlled).

return—code = 8197   The partner program abended or at least abended the conversation.

return–code = 0309   No data or status was received and the program is being cancelled.

Where the major code is 00 or 02 or 03, minor codes have the following meaning:

minor–code = 00   A turnaround was received. The local program can now send data.

minor–code = 01   No status was received.

minor–code = 08   The remote program has terminated the conversation.

Thus, in the following example, indicator 15 implies that the partner program is ready to receive, and indicator 35 implies that the partner program has terminated the conversation.

In DDS source:

```
A INDARA
A RCVTRNRND(15 'comment')
A RCVDETACH(35 'comment')
```

In COBOL source:

```
READ ICFFILE INDICATORS ARE CMNF–INDIC–AREA.
IF MAJ NOT = "03"
   PERFORM PROCESS–DATA.
IF CMNF–INDIC(15)
   GO TO SEND–DATA.
IF CMNF–INDIC(35)
   GO TO DONE–IT–ALL.
```

2.3.6 Terminating a conversation

A conversation can only be terminated normally by the TP that is in send state. However, the conversation can always be abended by either party.

OS/2

On the PC a conversation is terminated by issuing the verb MC_DEALLOCATE with the parameter type set to

AP_FLUSH. MC_DEALLOCATE naturally has two other parameters: TP_id and conv_id. The conversation is abended either by the program exiting without terminating the conversation normally, or by issuing the MC_DEALLOCATE verb with the parameter type set to AP_ABEND. If a verb returns with a return code set to AP_DE-ALLOC_ABEND indicating that the conversation had been abandoned from the other end, then no verbs need to be issued by the program: APPC will have freed all the resources that were being used by the conversation.

Thus for a normal deallocation you would issue the following:

```
APPC_MC_deallocate(tp_id, conv_id, AP_FLUSH, &lret);
```

and for an abnormal deallocation you would issue:

```
APPC_MC_deallocate(tp_id, conv_id, AP_ABEND, &lret);
```

CICS

Under CICS a conversation is terminated normally by issuing the command:

```
EXEC CICS SEND [CONVID(conv-id)]
               LAST
                                          END-EXEC
```

To terminate a conversation abnormally, issue the command:

```
EXEC CICS ISSUE ABEND [CONVID(conv-id)]
                                          END-EXEC
```

In either case, or when a conversation has been terminated by the remote TP, either normally or abnormally, you have to free the resources being used by issuing the command:

```
EXEC CICS FREE [CONVID(conv-id)]
                                          END-EXEC
```

It is possible to combine a SEND LAST with a SEND FROM(buffer), so that you can send data and terminate a conversation in one call:

```
EXEC CICS SEND [CONVID(conv-id)]
               FROM (buffer) LENGTH(length)
               LAST
                                    END-EXEC
```

However, this is not a good idea and should be avoided.

CPI-C

The function to call to deallocate a conversation is CMDEAL, which takes as parameters the conversation-ID and returns return-code. There is a conversation characteristic that needs to be set before the call, and that is the deallocate-type, which is set using the call CMSDT. Thus a normal deallocate would look like:

```
MOVE CM-DEALLOCATE-SYNC-LEVEL TO DEALLOCATE-TYPE
CALL "CMSDT" USING CONVERSATION-ID
               DEALLOCATE-TYPE
               RETURN-CODE.
CALL "CMDEAL" USING CONVERSATION-ID
               RETURN-CODE.
```

An abnormal termination of a conversation is achieved by the following calls:

```
MOVE CM-DEALLOCATE-ABEND TO DEALLOCATE-TYPE
CALL "CMSDT" USING CONVERSATION-ID
               DEALLOCATE-TYPE
               RETURN-CODE.
CALL "CMDEAL" USING CONVERSATION-ID
               RETURN-CODE.
```

AS/400

For an AS/400 program to terminate a conversation normally it must write to the ICF file using a format

containing the keyword DETACH. The system-supplied format $$SENDET provides this function.
   In DDS source:

```
      R DEALLOC
A 30                             DETACH
```

In the COBOL program:

```
    MOVE INDON TO CMNF-INDIC(30).
    WRITE ICFREC FORMAT IS "DEALLOC"
        INDICATORS ARE CMNF-INDIC-AREA.
    MOVE INOFF TO CMNF-INDIC(30).
```

To abend a conversation, the program has either to write to the ICF file specifying EOS(end of session), or simply to close the file without having first terminated the conversation. The system-provided format $$EOS provides this function.
   In DDS source:

```
      R ABEND
A 31                             EOS
```

In the COBOL program:

```
    MOVE INDON TO CMNF-INDIC(31).
    WRITE ICFREC FORMAT IS "ABEND"
        INDICATORS ARE CMNF-INDIC-AREA.
    MOVE INOFF TO CMNF-INDIC(31).
    CLOSE ICFFILE.
```

2.4 STATE DIAGRAMS

To make it clearer which verbs can be issued and what values can returned, it is useful to have the information presented in a state diagram. APPC is not complicated, as is indicated by the state diagram: there are very few states, especially for the essential subset.
   The state diagrams are given separately for each system. This is not because the logic is any different for the various systems, but merely to show the states and state transitions in terms of the functions as they are known on those

systems. Having said that the logic is the same on all the systems; you will notice that the state diagrams for CICS and the AS/400 have one more state defined than the diagrams for APPC on the PC and for CPI-C. This is because there is some cleanup processing required on terminated conversations on these two systems.

To reduce the amount of text in the diagrams themselves, and to increase the similarity between the diagrams, some abbreviations are used. The abbreviations in parentheses '(. . .)' are parameters passed to a function, those in curly brackets '{ . . . }' represent values returned. The meaning of these abbreviations is consistent across the diagrams, and they are explained in a system-specific fashion with each diagram.

To read the state diagrams, you have to think of the program as being in one of several states, such as send state or receive state. When a program is in a certain state only certain functions can legitimately be issued. If a function is issued when the program is in a state where that function cannot be issued then it returns a code indicating a state error. Issuing a function may cause the state of the program to change. The new state of the program resulting from issuing a function from a particular state is found by looking in the column headed by the current state number at the row labelled with the function being issued. If the entry is a number then that is the new state of the program. If it is an asterisk then the program remains in its current state, and if it is a hyphen then the function cannot be issued.

Some functions occur on several lines. This is because the new state of the program depends not only on the function being issued, but also on its parameters and possibly the values returned. In some instances, it is possible that while a function can be issued in a particular state, not all return codes are possible. To indicate this a slash '/' is used. An example of this is found in the state diagram for OS/2 (Fig. 2.2) where the function Receive_ and_wait can be issued while in send state (state 1), but it cannot return AP_DEALLOCATE_NORMAL.

Figs. 2.2–2.5 illustrate state diagrams for OS/2, CICS, CPI-C and AS/400, respectively.

Figure 2.2 State diagram for OS/2 APPC verbs

	States		
	0	1	2
Allocate	1	-	-
Receive_Allocate	2	-	-
Deallocate(F)	-	0	-
Deallocate(A)	-	0	0
Prepare_to_receive(F)	-	2	-
Receive_and_wait{da}	-	2	*
Receive_and_wait{se}	-	*	1
Receive_and_wait{dn}	-	/	0
Receive_and_wait{ab}	-	0	0
Receive_and_wait{er}	-	0	0
Send_data	-	*	-
Send_data{er}	-	0	-

Notes to Figure 2.2

States
0   Not allocated
1   Send
2   Receive

Matrix symbols
-     Verb cannot be issued in this state
/   Verb cannot return this in this state
*   Remains in this state
0–2   Number of next state

Parameter abbreviations (. . .)

A   Deallocate-type set to AP_ABEND.
F   Deallocate-type set to AP_FLUSH or sync level set to AP_FLUSH
    and deallocate-type set to AP_SYNC_LEVEL.

Returned-value abbreviations {. . .}

ab   DEALLOCATE_ABEND or ISSUE ABEND issue by partner,
     return-code = AP_DEALLOC_ABEND.
da   Data received, return-code = AP_OK, what-received =
     AP_DATA_COMPLETE or AP_DATA_INCOMPLETE
dn   Partner issued DEALLOCATE FLUSH or SEND LAST WAIT
     return-code = AP_DEALLOC_NORMAL.
er   Error on link or when allocating conversation or resource
     failure.
se   Partner issued a PREPARE_TO_RECEIVE or SEND INVITE
     WAIT or a RECEIVE, what-receive = AP_SEND.

Note that a conversation is in state 1, send, after issuing an
MC_ALLOCATE, and in state 2, receive, after issuing a
RECEIVE_ALLOCATE.

Figure 2.3 State diagram for CICS APPC verbs

	States			
	0	1	2	3
CONNECT PROCESS	1	-	-	-
(remotely started)	2	-	-	-
SEND LAST	-	3	-	-
ISSUE ABEND	-	3	3	-
FREE	-	-	-	0
SEND INVITE WAIT	-	2	-	-
RECEIVE {da}	-	2	*	-
RECEIVE {se}	-	*	1	-
RECEIVE {dn}	-	/	3	-
RECEIVE {ab}	-	3	3	-
RECEIVE {er}	-	3	3	-
SEND	-	*	-	-

Notes to Figure 2.3

States
0 Not allocated
1 Send
2 Receive
3 FREE pending

Matrix symbols
-    Verb cannot be issued in this state
/   Verb cannot return this in this state
*   Remains in this state
0–3 Number of next state

EIB variables set {. . .}

ab DEALLOCATE_ABEND or ISSUE ABEND issued by partner.
EIBFREE set, EIBERR set, EIBERRCD set to 0x08640000.
da Data received, EIBRECV set, EIBFREE and EIBERR not set.
dn Partner issued DEALLOCATE FLUSH or SEND LAST WAIT.
EIBFREE set, EIBERR not set.
er Error on link or when allocating conversation or resource
failure. TERMERR condition raised.
se Partner issued a PREPARE_TO_RECEIVE or SEND INVITE
WAIT or a RECEIVE. EIBRECV not set, EIBFREE and EIBERR
not set.

Note that a conversation is in state 1, send, after issuing an
CONNECT PROCESS, and in state 2, receive, after being
remotely started.

Figure 2.4 State diagram for CPI-C function calls

	States 0	States 1	States 2
CMALLC	1	-	-
CMACCP	2	-	-
CMDEAL (F)	-	0	-
CMDEAL (A)	-	0	0
CMPTR (F)	-	2	-
CMRCV {da}	-	2	*
CMRCV {se}	-	*	1
CMRCV {dn}	-	/	0
CMRCV {ab}	-	0	0
CMRCV {er}	-	0	0
CMSEND	-	*	-
CMSEND {er}	-	0	-

Notes to Figure 2.4

States
0   Not allocated
1   Send
2   Receive

Matrix symbols
-        Verb cannot be issued in this state
/   Verb cannot return this in this state
*   Remains in this state
0–2   Number of next state

Parameter abbreviations (. . .)

A   Deallocate-type set to CM–DEALLOCATE–ABEND.
F   Deallocate-type set to CM–DEALLOCATE–FLUSH or sync level set
      to CM–NONE and deallocate-type set to CM–DEALLOCATE–SYNC–
      LEVEL.

Returned-value abbreviations {. . .}

ab   DEALLOCATE–ABEND or ISSUE ABEND issued by partner,
       return–code = CM–DEALLOCATED–ABEND.
da   Only data received, return–code = CM–OK, data–received
       = CM–DATA–COMPLETE or CM–DATA–INCOMPLETE, status–
       received = CM–NO–STATUS–RECEIVED.
dn   Partner issued DEALLOCATE FLUSH or SEND LAST WAIT,
       return-code = CM–DEALLOCATED–NORMAL.
er   Error on link or when allocating conversation or resource
       failure.
se   Partner issued a PREPARE–TO–RECEIVE or SEND INVITE
       WAIT or a RECEIVE; status–receive = CM–SEND–
       RECEIVED.

Figure 2.5 State diagram for AS/400 APPC verbs

	States			
	0	1	2	3
EVOKE	1	-	-	-
(remotely started)	2	-	-	-
DETACH	-	3	-	-
EOS	-	0	0	0
INVITE	-	2	-	-
read {da}	-	2	*	-
read {se}	-	*	1	-
read {dn}	-	/	3	-
read {ab}	-	3	3	-
read {er}	-	3	3	-
Write	-	*	-	-

Notes to Figure 2.5

States

0 Not allocated

1 Send

2 Receive

3 Close or EOS pending

Matrix symbols

-       Verb cannot be issued in this state

/   Verb cannot return this in this state

*   Remains in this state

0–3   Number of next state

Returned value abbreviations {. . .}

ab DEALLOCATE–ABEND or write with ABEND issued by partner or partner abended: return–code = 8197.

da Only data received, partner issued write with no keywords: major–code = 00, 02, or 03; minor–code = 01.

dn Partner issued DEALLOCATE FLUSH or write with DETACH: major–code = 00, 02, or 03; minor–code = 08. RCVDETACH indicator set.

er Error on link or when allocating conversation or resource failure.

se Partner issued a PREPARE–TO–RECEIVE or write with INVITE or a RECEIVE or READ; major–code = 00, 02, or 03, minor–code = 00. RCVTRNRND indicator set.

2.5 SAMPLE APPC INTERACTIONS

Figs. 2.6–2.8 illustrate APPC interactions between a PC and CICS, CPI-C and AS/400, respectively.

Figure 2.6 (a) PC Sending data to CICS and receiving a reply

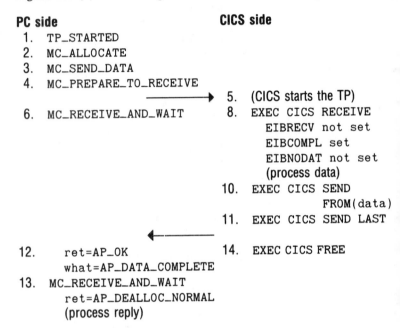

PC side		CICS side	
1.	`TP_STARTED`		
2.	`MC_ALLOCATE`		
3.	`MC_SEND_DATA`		
4.	`MC_PREPARE_TO_RECEIVE`		
	⟶	5.	(CICS starts the TP)
6.	`MC_RECEIVE_AND_WAIT`	8.	`EXEC CICS RECEIVE`
			`EIBRECV not set`
			`EIBCOMPL set`
			`EIBNODAT not set`
			(process data)
		10.	`EXEC CICS SEND`
			`FROM(data)`
		11.	`EXEC CICS SEND LAST`
	⟵		
12.	`ret=AP_OK`	14.	`EXEC CICS FREE`
	`what=AP_DATA_COMPLETE`		
13.	`MC_RECEIVE_AND_WAIT`		
	`ret=AP_DEALLOC_NORMAL`		
	(process reply)		

Notes to Figures 2.6a–2.6b

1. The PC program has to identify itself as a TP running on an LU.
2. Allocate the conversation. Two commands in CICS, one on the PC.
3. Send the data.
4. Reverse direction of conversation. This is a superfluous call as it is implied by the receive. Also on the CICS side it could be subsumed into the send data by putting the `INVITE WAIT` keywords in the previous command. This call is the first that actually causes data flow.
5. Remote program started. In some cases the program may already be running, waiting for incoming allocates.
6. Local program issues receive. This does not yet complete.
7. Remote PC program issues RECEIVE ALLOCATE to pick up conversation.

Figure 2.6 (b) CICS sending data to PC and receiving a reply

CICS side   **PC side**

```
 2.  EXEC CICS ALLOCATE SYSID(name)
 2.  EXEC CICS CONNECT PROCESS PROCNAME(name)
 2.  MOVE EIBRSRCE TO CONV_ID.
 3.  EXEC CICS SEND CONVID(CONV_ID) FROM(buffer)
 4.  EXEC CICS SEND CONVID(CONV_ID) INVITE WAIT
```
                          ─────────────▶   5. (Communications manager
```
 6.  EXEC CICS RECEIVE
```
                                               starts the program)
                                          7. RECEIVE_ALLOCATE
                                          8. MC_RECEIVE_AND_WAIT
                                                ret=AP_OK
                                                what=AP_DATA_COMPLETE
                                              (process data)
                                          9. MC_RECEIVE_AND_WAIT
                                                ret=AP_OK
                                                what=AP_SEND
                                         10. MC_SEND_DATA
                                         11. MC_DEALLOCATE
                                                type=AP_FLUSH

                       ◀─────────────

```
12.     EIBFREE set
        EIBCOMPL set
        EIBNODAT not set
14.  EXEC CICS FREE
     (process reply)
```

8. Remote program receives data. The CICS call also receives the SEND indicator.
9. The remote PC program has to issue a second receive to obtain the SEND indicator.
10. The remote program sends the reply, but nothing is transmitted yet.
11. The remote program deallocates the conversation. This causes the data to start flowing. This call could be subsumed into the send data in the CICS case.
12. The receive in the local program receives a reply.
13. The PC version of the local program has to issue a second receive to obtain the DEALLOCATE indicator.
14. The CICS programs have to call FREE to clean up.

Figure 2.7 (a) PC sending data to CPI-C and receiving a reply

PC side   **CPI-C side**
```
                                              1.   CALL XCIDRM
                                              2.   CALL XCWOE

  3.  TP_STARTED
  4.  MC_ALLOCATE
  5.  MC_SEND_DATA
  6.  MC_PREPARE_TO_RECEIVE
      ─────────────────────────►     7.   (XCWOE returns)
  8.  MC_RECEIVE_AND_WAIT            9.   CALL CMACCP
                                    10.   CALL CMRCV
                                             data-received = DATA-COMPLETE
                                             status-received = SEND-RECEIVED
                                          (process data)
                                    12.   CALL CMSEND
                                    13.   CALL CMSDT
                                             (CM-DEALLOC-FLUSH)
                                    13.   CALL CMDEAL

      ◄─────────────────────────
 14.      ret=AP_OK
          what=AP_DATA_COMPLETE
 15.  MC_RECEIVE_AND_WAIT
          ret=AP_DEALLOC_NORMAL
      (process reply)
```

Notes to Figures 2.7a–2.7b

1. The target program starts and identifies itself as a resource (TP).
2. The target program waits for something to happen.
3. The source program identifies itself.
4. Allocate the conversation, or initialize and allocate the conversation.
5. Send the data.
6. Turn the conversation around. This is a superfluous call as it is implied by the receive. This call is the first that actually causes data to flow.
7. The remote program is started or has received an event.
8. The local program issues a receive which does not yet complete.
9. The remote program accepts the allocate.

Figure 2.7 (b) CPI-C sending data to PC and receiving a reply

| CPI-C side | PC side |

CPI-C side

```
 4.  CALL CMINIT(sym-dest-name)
 4.  CALL CMALLC
 5.  CALL CMSEND(buffer)
 6.  CALL CMPTR
 8.  CALL CMRCV
```

PC side

```
 7.  (Communications manager
      starts the program)
 9.  RECEIVE_ALLOCATE
10.  MC_RECEIVE_AND_WAIT
      RET=AP_OK
      what=AP_DATA_COMPLETE
      (process data)
11.  MC_RECEIVE_AND_WAIT
      ret=AP_OK
      what=AP_SEND
12.  MC_SEND_DATA
13.  MC_DEALLOCATE
      type=AP_FLUSH
```

```
14.  return-code = CM-DEALLOCATED-NORMAL
      status-received = CM-NO-STATUS-RECEIVED
      data-received =CM-COMPLETE-DATA-RECEIVED
```

10. The remote program receives data. The CPI-C call also receives the SEND indicator.
11. The remote PC program has to issue a second receive to obtain the SEND indicator.
12. The remote program sends the reply, but nothing is transmitted yet.
13. The remote program deallocates the conversation. This causes the data to start flowing.
14. The receive in the local program receives a reply.
15. The PC version of the local program has to issue a second receive to obtain the DEALLOCATE indicator.

Figure 2.8 (a) PC sending data to AS/400 and receiving a reply

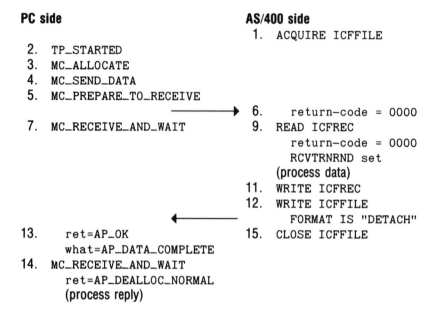

PC side

2.   TP_STARTED
3.   MC_ALLOCATE
4.   MC_SEND_DATA
5.   MC_PREPARE_TO_RECEIVE

7.   MC_RECEIVE_AND_WAIT

13.   ret=AP_OK
         what=AP_DATA_COMPLETE
14. MC_RECEIVE_AND_WAIT
         ret=AP_DEALLOC_NORMAL
     (process reply)

AS/400 side
1.   ACQUIRE ICFFILE

6.   return-code = 0000
9.   READ ICFREC
        return-code = 0000
        RCVTRNRND set
     (process data)
11.   WRITE ICFREC
12.   WRITE ICFFILE
        FORMAT IS "DETACH"
15.   CLOSE ICFFILE

Notes to Figures 2.8a–2.8b

1. The first action of an AS/400 program using APPC is to open and acquire the ICF file. This must be done by the receiving program so that it can accept incoming allocates.
2. The local PC program must identify itself to the communications manager.
3. Allocate the conversation.
4. Send the data.
5. Turn the conversation around. This is a superfluous call as it is implied by the receive. Also in the AS/400 side it could be subsumed into the send data by having the keyword INVITE in the format used. This is the first call that actually causes data to flow.
6. Remote program started, or returns from acquire.
7. Local program issues receive. This does not complete yet.
8. Remote PC program issues a RECEIVE ALLOCATE to pick up the conversation.

Figure 2.8 (b) AS/400 sending data to PC and receiving a reply

AS/400 side   **PC side**

```
 1.  OPEN ICFFILE
 3.  MOVE procname TO PGMNAME OF EVOKPGM-O
     WRITE ICFREC FORMAT IS "EVOKPGM"
 4.  WRITE ICFREC FORMAT IS "DATAFMT"
 5.  WRITE ICFREC FORMAT IS "INVITE"
```
                                       ⟶ 6. (communications manager

```
 7.  READ ICFREC                                  starts the program)
                                          8.  RECEIVE_ALLOCATE
                                          9.  MC_RECEIVE_AND_WAIT
                                                ret=AP_OK
                                                what=AP_DATA_COMPLETE
                                              (process data)
                                         10.  MC_RECEIVE_AND_WAIT
                                                ret=AP_OK
                                                what=AP_SEND
                                         11.  MC_SEND_DATA
                                         12.  MC_DEALLOCATE
                                                type=AP_FLUSH
```
⟵

```
13.  return-code = 0008
     RCVDETACH set
15.  CLOSE ICFFILE
     (process reply)
```

9. Remote program receives data. The AS/400 program also receives the SEND (RCVTRNRND) indicator.
10. The remote PC program has to issue a second receive to obtain the SEND indicator.
11. The remote program sends the reply, but nothing is sent yet.
12. The remote program deallocates the conversation. This causes the data to start flowing. This call could be subsumed into the send data in the AS/400 case by using a format that includes the keyword DETACH.
13. The receive in the local program receives the reply.
14. The PC version of the local program has to issue a second receive to obtain the DEALLOCATE indicator.
15. The AS/400 programs have to clean up by closing the ICF file or by issuing an EOS.

SUMMARY

The subset of APPC defined in this chapter is sufficient for many types of conversation, but omits in particular the support built into APPC for confirming and rejecting messages. Protocols can be built that do not need these additional features, but they often actually make life simpler. They are described in the next chapter.

REFERENCES FOR APPC

An introduction to APPC, GG24–1584–01.

SNA Programmers Reference Manual for LU Type 6.2, GC30–3084.

SNA Format and Protocol Reference Manual: Architecture Logic for LU Type 6.2, SC30–3269.

3 Further Programming for APPC

3.1 **INTRODUCTION**   The APPC features described in the previous chapter would be sufficient if the world were a perfect place. However, there is no provision in the subset described for things going wrong, with the exception of communications failures, which are almost always reported. But sometimes data faithfully transmitted can cause exception conditions: disks can be full, database records might not be there, there might be insufficient funds, etc.

One programming solution to these sorts of problem is to arrange that there must always be a reply to any request, and that the reply is always identified in some way as normal data or as an exception response. This is a reasonable method that works, and can be used, but there is a special way defined within APPC of indicating that a reply is an error message rather than normal data, and that is to issue the call SEND_ERROR before sending the message.

However, if this were the only use of SEND_ERROR, it would not be worth having: it has other more powerful uses. Consider, for instance, a pair of programs, one of which is sending a large amount of data to the other – a program update perhaps. Suppose the receiver runs out of disk space and is unable to write the data. It could wait until the sender stopped sending and then say 'Sorry, I couldn't cope with that', but that could be minutes later, and a lot of data could have been transmitted uselessly. SEND_ERROR can be issued even when a program is in receive state, and the error indicator is sent against the data flow and reported to the sender as a return code on the next verb issued. That is why SEND_ERROR exists.

51

Many interactions between programs are essentially one way: the only replies required are either a confirmation that everything worked or an error indicator. There is a mechanism built into APPC for just such a confirmation, and it comes in three different flavours:

1 A straightforward request for confirmation that the data sent so far has been processed.
2 A request for confirmation with a change direction.
3 A request for confirmation with a conditional termination of the conversation.

If the first of these is accepted, i.e. the receiver of the confirmation request confirms that the data has been processed, then the conversation continues in the same state as it was before the confirmation request was issued. This form of confirm could be used to hand over responsibility for chunks of data. For instance, if several files are being sent from one machine to another then between each file the two transaction programs could use CONFIRM/CONFIRMED to synchronize. After a good return code from CONFIRM, the sender can be confident that the receiver has the file safe on disk and so can delete its copy.

If the request for confirmation with change direction (CONFIRM–SEND) is accepted then the conversation is turned around, i.e. the program issuing the confirmation response is then in send state. This is the least useful and least used form of confirmation.

If the request for confirmation with conditional termination of the conversation (CONFIRM–DEALLOCATE) is accepted then the conversation is terminated. This is a widely used form of confirmation, and is frequently used when no confirmation is needed. It makes sense for a PC to obtain confirmation from a CICS transaction that a record has been added to a database successfully, rather than leaving the transaction in doubt, but it makes rather less sense for a CICS transaction to hang around waiting for confirmation that a record has been sent to a PC, if the data is just going to be displayed: if the data did not arrive the operator would ask for it again.

If, in response to any of these confirmation requests the receiving program issues a SEND_ERROR, then the direction of the conversation is left so that the program reporting a problem can send a message indicating why it could not accept the request for confirmation.

Note that CONFIRM confirms that the data has been processed, rather than that it has been delivered. There is not much point in confirming delivery: the communications protocol either delivers the data intact or returns an error. Typical interactions showing the use of CONFIRM/CONFIRMED and SEND_ERROR are given at the end of this chapter.

SEND_ERROR can be used on any conversation, but the CONFIRM/CONFIRMED handshaking can only be used on conversations that have been allocated specifying SYNC_LEVEL=CONFIRM.

3.2 CONVERSATIONS USING SYNC-LEVEL CONFIRM

OS/2

On the PC the conversation has to be started with an allocate verb specifying sync_level of CONFIRM, or the sync_level returned by the receive_allocate verb must be CONFIRM.

```
ret = APPC_MC_allocate(tp_id, partner_lu_name,
             mode_name,
             tpn, tpn_len,
             AP_WHEN_SESSION_ALLOCATED,
             AP_CONFIRM,
             AP_NONE,
             NULL, 0, NULL, 0,
             &conv_id,
             &ret2);
```

To request a straightforward confirmation without change direction, the PC issues the verb CONFIRM.

```
ret = APPC_MC_confirm(tp_id, conv_id, &rts, &ret2)
```

To request a confirm and turn the conversation around, the PC issues the verb prepare_to_receive with type SYNC_LEVEL. This prepare_to_receive must be issued explicitly as the prepare_to_receive implied by receive_and_wait is of type FLUSH.

```
ret = APPC_MC_prepare_to_receive(tp_id, conv_id,
                    AP_SYNC_LEVEL, AP_SHORT);
```

To request a conditional deallocate, the PC issues the verb `deallocate` with type SYNC_LEVEL.

```
APPC_MC_deallocate(tp_id, conv_id, AP_SYNC_LEVEL,
                                        &lret);
```

Each of these verbs returns AP_OK if the confirmation is forthcoming, and the state of the conversation is then advanced according to the type of confirmation that was requested. That is to say, after MC_CONFIRM returns AP_OK the state is send, after MC_PREPARE _TO_RECEIVE returns AP_OK the state is receive, and after MC_DEALLOCATE returns AP_OK the conversation has ceased to be.

A confirmation request is passed to the receiving process as a value of the what_received parameter returned from MC_RECEIVE_AND_WAIT:

AP_CONFIRM	Simple confirmation requested.
AP_CONFIRM_SEND	Confirm and change direction requested, i.e. to the receiving process confirm and then send.
AP_CONFIRM_DEALLOCATE	Conditional deallocate.

To accept a confirmation request, the PC issues the verb Confirmed:

```
ret = APPC_MC_confirmed(tp_id, conv_id, &rts, &ret2);
```

To reject a confirmation request, the PC issues the verb Send_Error.

```
ret = APPC_MC_send_error(tp_id,conv_id, &rts,&ret2);
```

The Send_Error verb can be issued at any time regardless of the current state of the conversation. This is reported to the partner program as a return code on the next verb it issues. That is, the send error indication can be sent against the flow of data in the conversation. The return code given on the verbs to indicate that the partner program has issued a SEND_ERROR is either AP_PROG_ERROR_PURGING if the program issuing the send error was in receive state, or AP_PROG_ERROR_NO_TRUNC if it was in send state or had a request for confirmation outstanding.

Note that it is possible for RECEIVE_AND_WAIT to return AP_PROG_ERROR_PURGING. This happens when both sides of the conversation are in receive state, which is not as unlikely as it sounds: if side A issues a RECEIVE_AND_WAIT and side B issues a SEND_DATA followed by a RECEIVE_AND_WAIT then both sides will be in receive state until side A receives the turnaround indicator.

CICS

Under CICS the conversation has to be started with the command

```
EXEC CICS CONNECT PROCESS . . . SYNCLEVEL(1)
                                    END-EXEC
```

or as the result of an incoming allocate specifying sync level of CONFIRM.

To request a straightforward confirmation without turning the conversation around, issue the command

```
EXEC CICS SEND CONFIRM
                                    END-EXEC
```

To request confirmation and turn the conversation around, issue the command

```
EXEC CICS SEND INVITE CONFIRM
                                    END-EXEC
```

To request a conditional deallocate, issue the command

```
EXEC CICS SEND LAST CONFIRM
                                    END-EXEC
```

Each of these commands returns with EIBERR not set if the confirmation is forthcoming, and then the state of the conversation is advanced according to the type of confirmation that was requested. That is to say, after issuing a SEND CONFIRM the conversation state is send, after SEND INVITE CONFIRM the state is receive, and after SEND LAST CONFIRM the state is free which means that only an EXEC CICS FREE is valid.

These requests for confirmation are passed to the receiving TP by setting EIBCONF after the RECEIVE command. The types of confirm are differentiated by the settings of EIBFREE and EIBRECV *after* the ISSUE CONFIRMATION command. These EIB variables, although not used by other CICS commands, are reset by them. They should therefore be tested or saved immediately after the APPC command has been issued.

EIBCONF set, EIBFREE not set, and EIBRECV set	Simple confirmation requested.
EIBCONF set, EIBFREE not set and EIBRECV not set	Confirm and change direction requested, i.e. the receiving process needs to issue a confirm and is then in send state.
EIBCONF set, EIBFREE set	Conditional deallocate.

To accept a confirmation request, the transaction program must issue the command

```
EXEC CICS ISSUE CONFIRMATION
                                      END-EXEC
```

To reject a confirmation request, the transaction program issues the command

```
EXEC CICS ISSUE ERROR
                                      END-EXEC
```

The send error command can be issued at any time regardless of the current state of the conversation. This is reported to the partner program as EIBERR being set and EIBERRCD being set to X'08890000' after the next

APPC command is issued. The send error indication can be sent against the flow of data in the conversation. CICS does not differentiate between a send error that was issued in send state and a send error issued in receive state.

CPI-C

Under CPI-C the conversation has to be started with a CMALLC function with the conversation characteristic sync-level set to CM-CONFIRM. This is done by issuing the call

```
MOVE CM-CONFIRM TO SYNC-LEVEL.
CALL "CMSSL" USING CONVERSATION-ID
                   SYNC-LEVEL
                   RETURN-CODE.
```

before the call to CMALLC. Alternatively, the conversation may be started by an incoming allocate specifying sync-level of CONFIRM.

To request a straightforward confirmation without change of direction, issue the function call CMCFM:

```
CALL "CMCFM" USING CONVERSATION-ID
                   RETURN-CODE.
```

To request a confirm and turn the conversation around, issue a prepare to receive with prepare-to-receive-type set to SYNC-LEVEL. This is done by issuing the following calls:

```
MOVE CM-PREP-TO-RECEIVE-SYNC-LEVEL TO PR-TYPE.
CALL "CMSPTR" USING CONVERSATION-ID
                    P2R-TYPE
                    RETURN-CODE.
CALL "CMPTR" USING CONVERSATION-ID
                   RETURN-CODE.
```

To request a conditional deallocate, issue a deallocate with deallocate-type set to CM-DEALLOCATE-SYNC-LEVEL. This is the default setting for deallocate-type, but can be emphasized by using the following calls:

```
MOVE CM-DEALLOCATE-SYNC-LEVEL TO DEALLOC-TYPE.
CALL "CMSDT" USING CONVERSATION-ID
                   DEALLOC-TYPE
                   RETURN-CODE.
CALL "CMDEAL" USING CONVERSATION-ID
                   RETURN-CODE.
```

Each of these verbs returns CM-OK if the confirmation is forthcoming and the state of the conversation is then advanced according to the type of confirmation that was requested. That is to say, after CMCF'M returns CM-OK the state is send, after CMPTR returns CM-OK the state is receive, and after CMDEAL returns CM-OK the conversation has ceased to be.

A confirmation request is passed to the receiving process as a value of the status_received parameter returned from CMRCV:

CM-CONFIRM-RECEIVED	Simple confirmation requested.
CM-CONFIRM-SEND-RECEIVED	Confirm and change direction requested, i.e. to the receiving process confirm and then send.
CM-CONFIRM-DEALLOC-RECEIVED	Conditional deallocate.

Remember that there may be data to process as well as the confirmation requests, and that the data returned at the same time as a confirmation request logically precede it.

To accept a confirmation request, issue the function CMCFMD. To reject a confirmation request, issue the function CMSERR.

The SEND-ERROR verb can be issued at any time regardless of the current state of the conversation. This is reported to the partner program as a return code on the next verb it issues. That is, the send error indication can be sent against the flow of data in the conversation. The return code given on the verbs to indicate that the partner program has issued a SEND-ERROR is either CM-PROGRAM-ERROR-PURGING if the program issuing the send error was in receive state, or CM–PROGRAM–ERROR–NO–TRUNC if it was in send state or with a request for confirmation outstanding.

In the case where the call to CMSERR follows a CMRCV that received both data and a SEND indicator, that is it returned data–received = CM–DATA–COMPLETE or CM–DATA–INCOMPLETE and status–received = CM–SEND–RECEIVED, CPI-C cannot tell if the send error refers to the processing of the incoming data, i.e. logically in receive state, or to problems in local processing related to sending a reply, i.e. logically in send state. This could be important: the programs might want to use CM–PROG–ERROR–PURGING to mean that the received data does not make sense, and CM–PROG–ERROR–NO–TRUNC to mean that the program encountered an error processing the data. It would be better to use an error code sent after the SEND–ERROR. There is a mechanism within CPI-C for the program to resolve this ambiguity. It can call CMSED to set the error direction to either CM–RECEIVE–ERROR or CM–SEND–ERROR. This is a pointless exercise if the partner program is CICS, as CICS does not differentiate between the two types of error.

AS/400

To be able to use the confirm/confirmed handshake on a conversation, an AS/400 program must start the conversation by issuing an evoke with the key-phrase SYNCLVL(*CONFIRM). There are no system-supplied formats for confirmation requests.

In the DDS source:

```
      R EVOKPGM
A 50                                 EVOKE(&PGMID)
A                                    SYNCLVL(*CONFIRM)
A           PGMID          10A  P
```

In the COBOL program:

```
01   ICFREC.
     COPY DDS-ALL-FORMATS OF SRCICF.
```

```
     OPEN I-O SRCICF.

     MOVE "tp-name" TO PGMID OF EVOKPGM-O.
     MOVE INDON TO CMNF-INDIC(50).
     WRITE ICFREC FORMAT IS "EVOKPGM"
        INDICATORS ARE CMNF-INDIC-AREA.
     MOVE INOFF TO CMNF-INDIC(50).
```

Alternatively, the conversation must have been started by the partner program with sync level set to confirm.

To request a straightforward confirmation without turning the conversation around, issue the command as follows.

In the DDS source:

```
     R CONFIRM
A 65                                  CONFIRM
```

In the COBOL program:

```
     MOVE INDON TO CMNF-INDIC(65).
     WRITE ICFREC FORMAT IS "CONFIRM"
        INDICATORS ARE CMNF-INDIC-AREA.
     MOVE INOFF TO CMNF-INDIC(65).
```

To request a confirmation and turn the conversation around, issue an invite with confirm.

In the DDS source:

```
R TURNCONF
   A  65                                  CONFIRM
   A                                      INVITE
```

In the COBOL program:

```
     MOVE INDON TO CMNF-INDIC(65).
     WRITE ICFREC FORMAT IS "TURNCONF"
        INDICATORS ARE CMNF-INDIC-AREA.
     MOVE INOFF TO CMNF-INDIC(65).
```

To request a conditional deallocate, issue a detach with confirm.

In the DDS source:

```
      R DETCONF
A 65                              CONFIRM
A                                DETACH
```

In the COBOL program:

```
MOVE INDON TO CMNF-INDIC(65).
WRITE ICFREC FORMAT IS "DETCONF"
    INDICATORS ARE CMNF-INDIC-AREA.
MOVE INOFF TO CMNF-INDIC(65).
```

Each of these commands returns with a return code of 0000 if the confirmation is forthcoming, and then the state of the conversation is advanced according to the type of confirmation issued. That is to say, after issuing a simple CONFIRM the state remains send, after a CONFIRM INVITE the conversation is turned around and is thus in receive state, and after a conditional deallocate DETACH CONFIRM the conversation ceases to be.

These requests for confirmation are passed to the receiving transaction program as return codes, and if the read specifies the appropriate indicators then they too are set.

Consider, for instance, the DDS source:

```
A INDARA
A RCVTRNRND(15 'comment')
A RCVDETACH(35 'comment')
A RCVCONFIRM(55 'comment')
```

and the COBOL source:

```
READ ICFFILE INDICATORS ARE CMNF-INDIC-AREA.
```

With the program fragment given above the confirmation requests are returned as follows:

Major-code 00, 02, or 03, minor-code 15, RCVCONFIRM set, but not RCVTRNRND or RCVDETACH.	A simple confirmation was requested.

Major-code 00, 02, or 03, minor-code 14, RCVCONFIRM and RCVTRNRND set, but not RCVDETACH	Confirm and change direction requested. The receiving process should process any data received with this call, confirm and then send.
Major-code 00, 02, or 03, minor-code 1C, RCVCONFIRM and RCVDETACH set, but not RCVTRNRND	Conditional deallocate.

To accept a confirmation request the program must issue a confirmation response. This is done by writing to the ICF file using a format which contains the keyword RSPCONFIRM.

In the DDS source:

```
  R RSPCONF
A 70                              RSPCONFIRM
```

In the COBOL program:

```
MOVE INDON TO CMNF-INDIC(70).
WRITE INCFREC FORMAT IS "RSPCONF"
   INDICATORS ARE CMNF-INDIC-AREA.
MOVE INOFF TO CMNF-INDIC(70).
```

To reject a confirmation request the program can send an error indication.

In the DDS source:

```
  R REJECT
A 75                              FAIL
```

In the COBOL program:

```
MOVE INDON TO CMNF-INDIC(75).
WRITE ICFREC FORMAT IS "REJECT"
   INDICATORS ARE CMNF-INDIC-AREA.
MOVE INOFF TO CMNF-INDIC(75).
```

The send error command can be used at any time regardless of the conversation state. This is reported to the partner program as a return code of 83C7 or 83C9. 83C7 is returned if the program issuing the error was in send state, and 83C9 is returned if the issuing program was in receive state. The program receiving notification of an error can arrange for an indicator to be set for either of these conditions by including the following line in the DDS source for the ICF file:

```
A RCVFAIL(85 'comment')
```

3.3 APPC MISCELLANEOUS FEATURES

There are a few features of APPC that have not yet been covered. These are as follows:

- Request-to-send.
- Test for request-to-send received.
- Flush.
- Receive immediate.

3.3.1 Request-to-send

Request-to-send is, in some ways, similar to send error in that a signal is transmitted against the main flow of data. However, it is different from send error in that the sole effect of issuing a request-to-send is that a flag is raised at the receiving end. Issuing a request-to-send never affects the conversation state, neither does it disrupt the flow of data. It is just as if one program has raised its hand to ask to be allowed to speak. That the partner has issued a request-to-send is indicated to the program at most once by setting a flag after the next APPC call made. If the partner issues a request-to-send before the program issues an APPC call, then the effect is that the request-to-send flag is raised on the next call only. That is to say, the extra request to sends are ignored.

OS/2

In OS/2 you issue the verb `MC_request_to_send` to send the request, and it is the `request_to_send_received` parameter that is set if a request-to-send has been received. There is a special call that does nothing except return this flag `MC_test_request_to_send`:

```
ret = APPC_MC_request_to_send(tp_id, conv_id, &lret);
```

To test for request-to-send you can issue the verb:

```
if (APPC_MC_test_RTS(tp_id, conv_id, &lret) == AP_OK)
{
  /*program has received RTS.*/
  }
```

CICS

In CICS you issue the command

```
EXEC CICS ISSUE SIGNAL END-EXEC.
```

to send the request to send, and the EIB variable EIBSIG is set after an APPC command if a request-to-receive has been received.

CPI-C

With CPI-C you issue the function call CMRTS to send a request-to-send. The parameter request-to-send-received is set if a request-to-send has been received. There is a special function CMTRTS that does nothing except return this flag.

To send a request-to-send:

```
CALL "CMRTS" USING CONVERSATION-ID
                   RETURN-CODE.
```

To test for a request-to-send:

```
CALL "CMTRTS" USING CONVERSATION-ID
                    RTS-RECEIVED
                    RETURN-CODE.
IF RTS-RECEIVED = CM-REQ-TO-SEND-RECEIVED
*    PARTNER PROGRAM SENT RTS
```

AS/400

An AS/400 program indicates that it wants to send by

writing to the ICF file using a format with the RQSWRT keyword.

In the DDS source:

```
    R RTS
A 88                              RQSWRT
```

In the COBOL program:

```
MOVE INDON TO CMNF-INDIC(88).
WRITE ICFREC FORMAT IS "RTS"
   INDICATORS ARE CMNF-INDIC-AREA.
MOVE INOFF TO CMNF-INDIC(88).
```

In the partner program, notification that a request-to-send has been received is put in the I/O feedback communications-dependent section. For instance, whether a RTS has been received can be tested for as follows:

```
IF RQSWRT OF IO-FDBK = 1 THEN
      GO TO LET-THEM-SPEAK.
```

3.3.2 Flush

APPC is a 'lazy' architecture: it will not send anything from one program to another sooner than it has to. It accumulates in its buffers the data sent until a confirmation, deallocation or change direction is requested. There is a way of circumventing some of this buffering, and that is by issuing the instruction Flush.

OS/2

In OS/2 this is done by issuing the verb flush:

```
APPC_MC_flush(tp_id, conv_id, &lret);
```

CICS

Under CICS the buffers are flushed by issuing the command:

```
EXEC CICS SEND WAIT END-EXEC.
```

CPI-C

With CPI-C this done by issuing the functional call CMFLUS:

```
CALL "CMFLUS" USING CONVERSATION-ID RETURN-CODE.
```

AS/400

An AS/400 program can force any buffered data to be sent by issuing the following command
In the DDS source:

```
    R FLUSH
A 89                              FRCDTA
```

In the COBOL program

```
MOVE INDON TO CMNF-INDIC(89).
WRITE ICFREC FORMAT IS "FLUSH"
    INDICATORS ARE CMNF-INDIC-AREA.
MOVE INOFF TO CMNF-INDIC(89).
```

3.3.3 RECEIVE_IMMEDIATE

In some environments it is also possible to check if there is anything to receive, and to receive what there is without having to wait for something to arrive.

OS/2

In OS/2 this is achieved by using the MC_RECEIVE_IMMEDIATE verb. This can be used anywhere that a MC_RECEIVE_AND_WAIT verb is valid, except that receive immediate does *not* imply prepare-to-receive if used in send state. It also has an additional possible return code: AP_UNSUCCESSFUL, meaning that there was nothing to receive.

```
ret = APPC_MC_receive_immediate(tp_id, conv_id,
        buffer, sizeof(buffer),
        &reclen, &what,
        &rts, &lret);
```

CPI-C

With CPI-C there is a conversation characteristic that can be set that alters the behaviour of the receive function CMRCV. CMRCV by default waits if there is nothing to receive, but if receive-type is set to CM-RECEIVE-IMMEDIATE by issuing the function call

```
MOVE CM-RECEIVE-IMMEDIATE TO RECEIVE-TYPE.
CALL "CMSRT" USING CONVERSATION-ID
            RECEIVE-TYPE
            RETURN-CODE.
```

then CMRCV returns with return-code set to CM-UNSUCCESSFUL if there is nothing to receive.

Neither CICS nor the AS/400 have an equivalent to receive-immediate.

3.4 EBCDIC AND ASCII

IBM mainframe computers use a different character set to that used by PCs. It is obviously essential that for successful communications between a PC program and a CICS transaction program they need to agree the character set to be used for data transfer.

Conversion to and from EBCDIC are not only necessary for messages exchanged with the mainframe: some of the parameters passed to the APPC verbs also have to be in EBCDIC. Table 3.1 indicates which should be in EBCDIC, and which in ASCII.

Table 3.1 Parameters and their character sets

Parameters	EBCDIC or ASCII
LU_ALIAS	ASCII
MODE_NAME	EBCDIC
PARTNER_LU_ALIAS	ASCII
PASSWORD	EBCDIC
TP_NAME	EBCDIC
USER_ID	EBCDIC

The communications manager on the PC offers a function to convert between EBCDIC and ASCII, and vice versa. The use of this facility is illustrated in the code fragment shown:

```
errmsglen = strlen("PCAP001: DATA INCONSISTENT");
convert(SV_ASCII_TO_EBCDIC, SV_G, errmsglen,
            "PCAP001: DATA INCONSISTENT", errmsg);
```

3.5 STATE DIAGRAMS

To make it clearer which verbs can be issued and what values can be returned it is useful to have a table or state diagram. APPC is not complicated, as is indicated by the state diagram: there are very few states, especially for this subset.

The state diagrams are given separately for each system. This is not because the logic is any different for the various systems, but merely to show the states and state transitions in terms of the functions as they are known on those systems. Having said that the logic is the same on all the systems, you will notice that the state diagrams for CICS and the AS/400 have one more state defined than the diagrams for APPC on the PC and for CPI-C. This is because there is some cleanup processing required on terminated conversations on these two systems.

To reduce the amount of text in the diagrams themselves, and to increase the similarity between the diagrams, some abbreviations are used. The abbreviations in parentheses '(. . .)' are parameters passed to a function, and those in curly brackets '{. . .}' represent values returned. The meaning of these abbreviations is consistent across the diagrams, and they are explained in a system-specific fashion with each diagram.

Figs. 3.1–3.4 show the state diagrams for OS/2, CICS, CPI-C and AS/400, respectively.

Figure 3.1 State diagram for OS/2 APPC verbs

	States					
	0	1	2	3	4	5
Allocate	1	-	-	-	-	-
Receive_Allocate	2	-	-	-	-	-
Confirm{ok}	-	*	-	-	-	-
Confirm{ep}	-	2	-	-	-	-
Confirmed	-	-	-	2	1	0
Deallocate(F)	-	0	-	-	-	-
Deallocate(A)	-	0	0	0	0	0
Deallocate(C){ok}	-	0	-	-	-	-
Deallocate(C){er}	-	0	-	-	-	-
Deallocate(C){ep}	-	2	-	-	-	-
Flush	-	*	-	-	-	-
Prepare_to_receive(F)	-	2	-	-	-	-
Prepare_to_receive(C){ok}	-	2	-	-	-	-
Prepare_to_receive(C){er}	-	0	-	-	-	-
Prepare_to_receive(C){ep}	-	2	-	-	-	-
Receive_. . .{da}	-	(2)	*	-	-	-
Receive_. . .{se}	-	(*)	1	-	-	-
Receive_. . .{co}	-	(3)	3	-	-	-
Receive_. . .{cs}	-	(4)	4	-	-	-
Receive_. . .{cd}	-	(5)	5	-	-	-
Receive_. . .{dn}	-	/	0	-	-	-
Receive_. . .{ab}	-	(0)	0	-	-	-
Receive_. . .{er}	-	(0)	0	-	-	-
Receive_. . .{ep}	-	(2)	*	-	-	-
Receive_immediate{un}	-	-	*	-	-	-
Request_to_send	-	-	*	*	*	*
Send_data{ok}	-	*	-	-	-	-
Send_data{er}	-	0	-	-	-	-
Send_data{ep}	-	2	-	-	-	-
Send_error{ok}	-	*	1	1	1	1
Send_error{er}	-	0	0	0	0	0
Send_error{dn}	-	/	0	/	/	/
Send_error{ep}	-	2	*	/	/	/
Test_RTS	*	-	*	*	*	*

Notes to Figure 3.1

States		*Matrix symbols*
0	Not allocated	- Verb cannot be issued in this state.
1	Send	
2	Receive	/ Verb cannot return this in this state.
3	Confirm	
4	Confirm Send	* Remains in this state.
5	Confirm Receive	0–5 Number of next state.

Numbers in brackets only valid for
RECEIVE_AND_WAIT.

Parameter abbreviations (. . .)

A   TYPE(ABEND)
F   TYPE(FLUSH)
C   TYPE(SYNC_LEVEL)

Returned-value abbreviations {. . .}

ab   DEALLOCATE_ABEND or ISSUE ABEND issued by partner,
     return_code = AP_DEALLOC_ABEND.
cd   Partner issued DEALLOCATE SYNC_LEVEL = CONFIRM or
     SEND LAST CONFIRM, return_code = AP_OK,
     what_received = AP_CONFIRM_DEALLOCATE.
co   CONFIRM or SEND CONFIRM issued by partner,
     return_code = AP_OK,
     what_received = AP_CONFIRM_WHAT_RECEIVED.
cs   Partner issued PREPARE_TO_RECEIVE
     SYNC_LEVEL(CONFIRM) or SEND INVITE CONFIRM
     return_code = AP_OK,
     what_received = AP_CONFIRM_SEND.
da   Only data received, return_code = AP_OK,
     what_received = AP_DATA_COMPLETE or
     AP_DATA_INCOMPLETE.
dn   Partner issued DEALLOCATE FLUSH or SEND LAST WAIT,
     return_code = AP_DEALLOC_NORMAL.
ep   Partner issued a SEND_ERROR or ISSUE ERROR,
     return_code = AP_PROG_ERROR_NO_TRUNC or
     AP_PROG_ERROR_PURGING.
er   Program error, resource failure or allocate failure.
se   Partner issued PREPARE_TO_RECEIVE FLUSH or
     SEND INVITE WAIT, return_code = AP_OK,
     what_received = AP_SEND.
un   There was nothing to receive, return–code =
     AP_UNSUCCESSFUL.

Figure 3.2 State diagram for CICS APPC commands

	States						
	0	1	2	3	4	5	6
CONNECT PROCESS	1	-	-	-	-	-	-
(remotely started)	2	-	-	-	-	-	-
SEND CONFIRM. not EIBERR	-	*	-	-	-	-	-
SEND CONFIRM. EIBERR set	-	2	-	-	-	-	-
ISSUE CONFIRMATION	-	-	-	2	1	6	-
SEND LAST	-	6	-	-	-	-	-
ISSUE ABEND	-	6	6	6	6	6	-
SEND LAST CONFIRM. not EIBERR	-	6	-	-	-	-	-
SEND LAST CONFIRM. TERMERR	-	6	-	-	-	-	-
SEND LAST CONFIRM. EIBERR set	-	2	-	-	-	-	-
WAIT	-	*	-	-	-	-	-
SEND INVITE WAIT	-	2	-	-	-	-	-
SEND INVITE CONFIRM. not EIBERR	-	2	-	-	-	-	-
SEND INVITE CONFIRM. TERMERR	-	6	-	-	-	-	-
SEND INVITE CONFIRM. EIBERR	-	2	-	-	-	-	-
RECEIVE {da}	-	2	*	-	-	-	-
RECEIVE {se}	-	*	1	-	-	-	
RECEIVE {co}	-	3	3	-	-	-	-
RECEIVE {cs}	-	4	4	-	-	-	-
RECEIVE {cd}	-	5	5	-	-	-	-
RECEIVE {dn}	-	/	6	-	-	-	-
RECEIVE {ab}	-	6	6	-	-	-	-
RECEIVE TERMERR	-	6	6	-	-	-	-
RECEIVE {ep}	-	2	*	-	-	-	-
ISSUE SIGNAL	-	-	*	*	*	*	-
SEND FROM(buffer). not EIBERR	-	*	-	-	-	-	-
SEND FROM(buffer). TERMERR	-	6	-	-	-	-	-
SEND FROM(buffer). EIBERR set	-	2	-	-	-	-	-
ISSUE ERROR. not EIBERR, not EIBFREE	-	*	1	1	1	1	-
ISSUE ERROR. TERMERR	-	6	6	6	6	6	-
ISSUE ERROR. not EIBERR, EIBFREE set	-	/	6	/	/	/	-
ISSUE ERROR. EIBERR set, EIBFREE set	-	2	*	/	/	/	-
FREE	-	-	-	-	-	-	0

Notes to Figure 3.2

States		*Matrix symbols*	
0	Not allocated	-	Verb cannot be issued in this state.
1	Send		
2	Receive	/	Verb cannot return this in this state.
3	Confirm		
4	Confirm send	*	Remains in this state.
5	Confirm receive	0–6	Number of next state.
6	Free		

EIB variables returned {...}

ab   DEALLOCATE ABEND or ISSUE ABEND issued by partner,
EIBFREE set, EIBERR set, EIBERRCD = X'08640000'.

cd   Partner issued DEALLOCATE SYNC_LEVEL(CONFIRM) or
SEND LAST CONFIRM, EIBCONF set, EIBERR not set,
EIBFREE will be set after ISSUE CONFIRMATION.

co   CONFIRM or SEND CONFIRM issued by partner, EIBCONF set,
not EIBFREE, not EIBERR, EIBRECV set.

cs   Partner issued
PREPARE_TO_RECEIVE_SYNC_LEVEL(CONFIRM) or
SEND INVITE CONFIRM.
EIBCONF set, not EIBFREE, not EIBERR, not EIBRECV.

da   Only data received not EIBCONF, not EIBFREE, not EIBERR,
EIBRECV set.

dn   Partner issued DEALLOCATE FLUSH or SEND LAST WAIT
not EIBCONF, EIBFREE set, not EIBERR

ep   Partner issued a SEND_ERROR or ISSUE ERROR.
EIBERR set, EIBERRCD = X'08890000', EIBRECV set.

se   Partner issued PREPARE_TO_RECEIVE FLUSH or SEND
INVITE WAIT,
not EIBCONF, not EIBFREE, not EIBRECV, not EIBERR.

TERMERR   TERMERR condition is raised. EIBERR set. EIBERRCD
provides further information.

Figure 3.3 State diagram for CPI-C functions

	States					
	0	1	2	3	4	5
CMALLC	1	-	-	-	-	-
CMACCP	2	-	-	-	-	-
CMCFM{ok}	-	*	-	-	-	-
CMCFM{ep}	-	2	-	-	-	-
CMCFMD	-	-	-	2	1	0
CMDEAL(F)	-	0	-	-	-	-
CMDEAL(A)	-	0	0	0	0	0
CMDEAL(C){ok}	-	0	-	-	-	-
CMDEAL(C){er}	-	0	-	-	-	-
CMDEAL(C){ep}	-	2	-	-	-	-
CMFLUS	-	*	-	-	-	-
CMPTR(F)	-	2	-	-	-	-
CMPTR(C){ok}	-	2	-	-	-	-
CMPTR(C){er}	-	0	-	-	-	-
CMPTR(C){ep}	-	2	-	-	-	-
CMRCV{da}	-	(2)	*	-	-	-
CMRCV{se}	-	(*)	1	-	-	-
CMRCV{co}	-	(3)	3	-	-	-
CMRCV{cs}	-	(4)	4	-	-	-
CMRCV{cd}	-	(5)	5	-	-	-
CMRCV{dn}	-	/	0	-	-	-
CMRCV{ab}	-	(0)	0	-	-	-
CMRCV{er}	-	(0)	0	-	-	-
CMRCV{ep}	-	(2)	*	-	-	-
CMRCV{un}	-	-	*	-	-	-
CMRTS	-	-	*	*	*	*
CMSEND{ok}	-	*	-	-	-	-
CMSEND{er}	-	0	-	-	-	-
CMSEND{ep}	-	2	-	-	-	-
CMSERR{ok}	-	*	1	1	1	1
CMSERR{er}	-	0	0	0	0	0
CMSERR{dn}	-	/	0	/	/	/
CMSERR{ep}	-	2	*	/	/	/
CMTRTS	*	-	*	*	*	*

Notes to Figure 3.3

States		*Matrix symbols*	
0	Not allocated	-	Verb cannot be issued in this state.
1	Send	/	Verb cannot return this in this state.
2	Receive	*	Remains in this state.
3	Confirm	0–5	Number of next state.
4	Confirm send		Numbers in brackets only valid for
5	Confirm receive		CMRCV with receive-type set to CM–RECEIVE–AND–WAIT.

Parameter abbreviations (. . .)

A Deallocate-type set to CM–ABEND.
F Deallocate-type set to CM–DEALLOCATE–FLUSH or prepare-to-receive-type set to CM–PREPARE–TO–RECEIVE–FLUSH or sync-level set to CM–NONE and ***-type set to **-SYNC–LEVEL.
C Sync-level set to CM–CONFIRM and deallocate-type CM–DEALLOCATE–SYNC–LEVEL or prepare-to-receive-type set to CM–PREPARE–TO–RECEIVE–SYNC–LEVEL.

Returned-value abbreviations { . . .}

ab DEALLOCATE–ABEND or ISSUE ABEND issued by partner, return–code = CM–DEALLOCATE–ABEND.
cd Partner issued DEALLOCATE SYNC–LEVEL(CONFIRM) or SEND LAST CONFIRM, return code = CM–OK, status–received = CM–CONFIRM–DEALLOC–RECEIVED.
co CONFIRM or SEND CONFIRM issued by partner, return–code = CM–OK, status–received = CM–CONFIRM–RECEIVED.
cs Partner issued PREPARE–TO–RECEIVE SYNC–LEVEL(CONFIRM) or SEND INVITE CONFIRM, return–code = CM–OK, status–received = CM–CONFIRM–SEND–RECEIVED.
da Only data received, return–code = CM–OK, status–received = CM–NO–STATUS–RECEIVED.
dn Partner issued DEALLOCATE FLUSH or SEND LAST WAIT, return–code = CM–DEALLOCATE–NORMAL.
ep Partner issued a SEND–ERROR or ISSUE ERROR, return–code = CM–PROGRAM–ERROR–NO–TRUNC or CM–PROGRAM–ERROR–PURGING.
er Error on link or when allocating the conversation, or resource failure.
se Partner issued PREPARE–TO–RECEIVE FLUSH or SEND INVITE WAIT, return–code = CM–OK, status–received = CM–SEND–RECEIVED.
un There was nothing to receive, return–code = CM–UNSUCCESSFUL.

Figure 3.4 State diagram for AS/400 APPC commands

	States						
	0	1	2	3	4	5	6
EVOKE	1	-	-	-	-	-	-
(remotely started)	2	-	-	-	-	-	-
CONFIRM ret-code = 0000	-	*	-	-	-	-	-
CONFIRM ret-code NOT = 0000	-	2	-	-	-	-	-
RSPCONFIRM	-	-	-	2	1	6	-
DETACH	-	6	-	-	-	-	-
EOS	-	0	0	0	0	0	0
DETACH CONFIRM ret-code=0000	-	6	-	-	-	-	-
DETACH CONFIRM {er}	-	6	-	-	-	-	-
DETACH CONFIRM {ep}	-	2	-	-	-	-	-
FRCDTA	-	*	-	-	-	-	-
INVITE	-	2	-	-	-	-	-
INVITE CONFIRM ret-code=0000	-	2	-	-	-	-	-
INVITE CONFIRM {er}	-	6	-	-	-	-	-
INVITE CONFIRM {ep}	-	2	-	-	-	-	-
read {da}	-	2	*	-	-	-	-
read {se}	-	*	1	-	-	-	-
read {co}	-	3	3	-	-	-	-
read {cs}	-	4	4	-	-	-	-
read {cd}	-	5	5	-	-	-	-
read {dn}	-	/	6	-	-	-	-
read {ab}	-	6	6	-	-	-	-
read {er}	-	6	6	-	-	-	-
read {ep}	-	2	*	-	-	-	-
RQSWRT	-	-	*	*	*	*	-
write ret-code =0000	-	*	-	-	-	-	-
write {er}	-	6	-	-	-	-	-
write {ep}	-	2	-	-	-	-	-
FAIL ret-code = 0000	-	*	1	1	1	1	-
FAIL {er}	-	6	6	6	6	6	-
FAIL {dn}	-	/	6	/	/	/	-
FAIL {ep}	-	2	*	/	/	/	-

Notes to Figure 3.4

States		*Matrix symbols*	
0	Not allocated	-	Verb cannot be issued in this state.
1	Send		
2	Receive	/	Verb cannot return this in this state.
3	Confirm		
4	Confirm send	*	Remains in this state.
5	Confirm receive	0–6	Number of next state.
6	EOS pending		

Return codes and indicators set on return {. . .}

ab   DEALLOCATE ABEND or EOS issued by partner, `return-code`
     = 8197.

cd   Partner issued DEALLOCATE SYNC-LEVEL(`CONFIRM`) or
     DETACH CONFIRM, `major-code` = 00, 01, or 03, `minor-code` = 1C. RCVCONFIRM and RCVDETACH set.

co   CONFIRM issued by partner, `major-code` = 00, 01, or 03,
     `minor-code` = 15. RCVCONFIRM set.

cs   Partner issued PREPARE_TO_RECEIVE
     SYNC_LEVEL(`CONFIRM`) or SEND INVITE CONFIRM,
     `major-code` = 00, 01, or 03, `minor-code` = 14.
     RCVCONFIRM and RCVTRNRND set.

da   Only data received, `major-code` = 00, 01, or 03, `minor-code` = 01.

dn   Partner issued DEALLOCATE FLUSH or DETACH, `major-code`
     = 00, 01, or 03, `minor-code` = 08, RCVDETACH set.

ep   Partner issued a SEND_ERROR or FAIL, `error-code` = 83C7
     or 83C9. RCVFAIL set.

er   Error on link or when allocating the conversation, or resource
     failure, `error-code` is set.

se   Partner issued PREPARE_TO_RECEIVE FLUSH or INVITE,
     `major-code` = 00, 01, or 03, `minor-code` = 00,
     RCVTRNRND set.

3.6   MORE SAMPLE APPC INTERACTIONS   Figs. 3.5–3.10 illustrate further APPC interactions for the four systems under consideration.

Figure 3.5 (a) PC sending data to CICS and receiving a confirmation

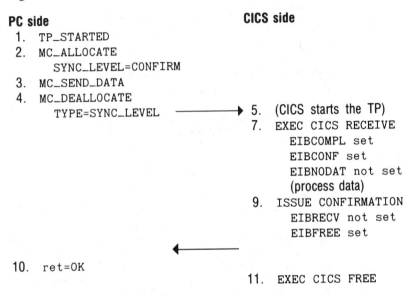

PC side

1. `TP_STARTED`
2. `MC_ALLOCATE`
     `SYNC_LEVEL=CONFIRM`
3. `MC_SEND_DATA`
4. `MC_DEALLOCATE`
     `TYPE=SYNC_LEVEL` ⟶

10. `ret=OK`

CICS side

5. (CICS starts the TP)
7. `EXEC CICS RECEIVE`
     `EIBCOMPL set`
     `EIBCONF set`
     `EIBNODAT not set`
     (process data)
9. `ISSUE CONFIRMATION`
     `EIBRECV not set`
     `EIBFREE set`

11. `EXEC CICS FREE`

Figure 3.5 (b) CICS sending data to PC and receiving a confirmation

CICS side   **PC side**

```
  2.   EXEC CICS ALLOCATE SYSID(name)
  2.   EXEC CICS CONNECT PROCESS SYNCLEVEL(1)
       MOVE EIBRSRCE TO CONV-ID.
  3.   EXEC CICS SEND FROM(buffer)
  4.   EXEC CICS SEND LAST CONFIRM
                                        ──────▶  5.   (communications manager
                                                       starts the program)
                                                 6.   RECEIVE_ALLOCATE
                                                 7.   MC_RECEIVE_AND_WAIT
                                                          ret=OK
                                                          what=DATA_COMPLETE
                                                       (process data)
                                                 8.   MC_RECEIVE_AND_WAIT
                                                          ret=OK
                                                          what=CONFIRM_DEALLOCATE
                                                 9.   MC_CONFIRMED
                                ◀──────────────
 10.       EIBERR not set
 11.   EXEC CICS FREE
```

Notes to Figures 3.5a–3.5b

1. The PC program has to identify itself as a TP running on an LU.
2. Allocate the conversation. Two commands in CICS, one on the PC.
3. Send the data.
4. Conditionally deallocate the conversation. In the CICS version it could be subsumed into the send data by putting the LAST CONFIRM keywords in the previous command. This is the first command that actually causes data to be sent.
5. Remote program started. In some cases the program may already be running, waiting for incoming allocates.
6. Remote PC program issues RECEIVE ALLOCATE to pick up the conversation.
7. Remote program receives data. The CICS call also receives the SEND indicator.
8. The remote PC program has to issue a second receive to obtain the SEND indicator.
9. The remote PC issues a confirmation to indicate that it has successfully processed the data.
10. The deallocate command issued by the sending program returns with no error indication. It now knows that the data has been processed.
11. The CICS TPs have to issue a FREE to clean up.

Figure 3.6 (a) PC sending data to CICS and receiving an error reply

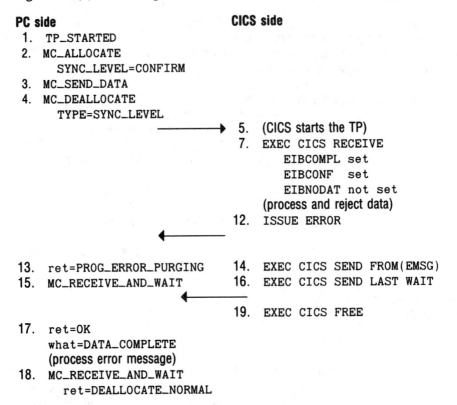

PC side

1. `TP_STARTED`
2. `MC_ALLOCATE`
   `SYNC_LEVEL=CONFIRM`
3. `MC_SEND_DATA`
4. `MC_DEALLOCATE`
   `TYPE=SYNC_LEVEL`

13. `ret=PROG_ERROR_PURGING`
15. `MC_RECEIVE_AND_WAIT`

17. `ret=OK`
    `what=DATA_COMPLETE`
    (process error message)
18. `MC_RECEIVE_AND_WAIT`
    `ret=DEALLOCATE_NORMAL`

CICS side

5. (CICS starts the TP)
7. `EXEC CICS RECEIVE`
   `EIBCOMPL set`
   `EIBCONF  set`
   `EIBNODAT not set`
   (process and reject data)
12. `ISSUE ERROR`

14. `EXEC CICS SEND FROM(EMSG)`
16. `EXEC CICS SEND LAST WAIT`

19. `EXEC CICS FREE`

Notes to Figures 3.6a–6b

12. The remote program does not like the data so sends an error indication.
13. The deallocate in the sending program returns with an error.
14. The remote program sends an error message to explain what it does not like.
15. The local program issues a receive to make the error message forthcoming.
16. The remote program issues a deallocate type flush. This causes the error message to be sent and unconditionally terminates the conversation. The program can terminate before the error message reaches the local program.
17. The receive issued by the local program returns with the error message, and in the case of the CICS version also with notification that the conversation has terminated.
18. The PC version of the local program has to issue another receive to obtain the deallocation notification.
19. The CICS programs have to call FREE to clean up.

Figure 3.6 (b) CICS sending data to PC and receiving an error reply

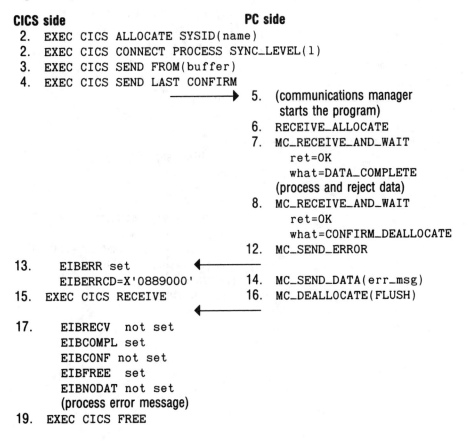

CICS side

2. `EXEC CICS ALLOCATE SYSID(name)`
2. `EXEC CICS CONNECT PROCESS SYNC_LEVEL(1)`
3. `EXEC CICS SEND FROM(buffer)`
4. `EXEC CICS SEND LAST CONFIRM`

13. `EIBERR set`
     `EIBERRCD=X'0889000'`
15. `EXEC CICS RECEIVE`

17. `EIBRECV  not set`
     `EIBCOMPL set`
     `EIBCONF not set`
     `EIBFREE  set`
     `EIBNODAT not set`
     (process error message)
19. `EXEC CICS FREE`

PC side

5. (communications manager
    starts the program)
6. `RECEIVE_ALLOCATE`
7. `MC_RECEIVE_AND_WAIT`
       `ret=OK`
       `what=DATA_COMPLETE`
    (process and reject data)
8. `MC_RECEIVE_AND_WAIT`
       `ret=OK`
       `what=CONFIRM_DEALLOCATE`
12. `MC_SEND_ERROR`

14. `MC_SEND_DATA(err_msg)`
16. `MC_DEALLOCATE(FLUSH)`

Figure 3.7 (a) PC sending data to CPI-C and receiving a confirmation

PC side

CPI-C side
1.   CALL XCIDRM
2.   CALL XCWOE

3.   TP_STARTED
4.   MC_ALLOCATE
      SYNC_LEVEL=CONFIRM
5.   MC_SEND_DATA
6.   DEALLOCATE
      TYPE=SYNC_LEVEL   ⟶

7.   (XCWOE returns)
8.   CALL CMACCP
9.   CALL CMRCV
      data-received =
         CM-DATA-COMPLETE
      status-received =
         CM-CONFIRM-DEALLOC-RECEIVED
      return-code = CM-OK
   (process data)
11. CALL CMCFMD
  ⟵

12. ret=OK

Figure 3.7 (b) CPI-C sending data to PC and receiving a confirmation

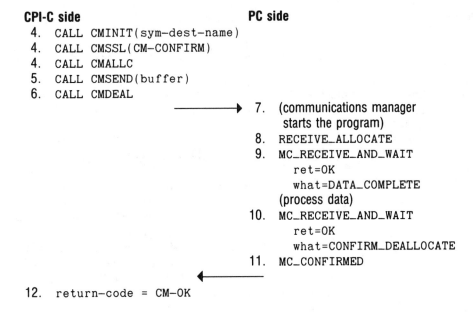

CPI-C side

```
 4.   CALL CMINIT(sym-dest-name)
 4.   CALL CMSSL(CM-CONFIRM)
 4.   CALL CMALLC
 5.   CALL CMSEND(buffer)
 6.   CALL CMDEAL
```

PC side

```
 7.   (communications manager
       starts the program)
 8.   RECEIVE_ALLOCATE
 9.   MC_RECEIVE_AND_WAIT
         ret=OK
         what=DATA_COMPLETE
       (process data)
10.   MC_RECEIVE_AND_WAIT
         ret=OK
         what=CONFIRM_DEALLOCATE
11.   MC_CONFIRMED
```

```
12.   return-code = CM-OK
```

Notes to Figures 3.7a–3.7b

1. The target program starts and identifies itself as a resource (TP).
2. The target program waits for something to happen.
3. The source program identifies itself.
4. Allocate the conversation, or initialize and allocate the conversation.
5. Send the data.
6. Conditionally deallocate the conversation.
7. The remote program is started or receives an event.
8. The remote program accepts the incoming allocate.
9. The remote program receives the data. The CPI-C call also receives the CONFIRM DEALLOCATE status return.
10. The remote PC program has to issue a second receive to achieve the CONFIRM DEALLOCATE status return.
11. The remote program issues a confirmation to indicate that it has successfully processed the data.
12. The deallocate in the local program returns OK. The local program now knows that the data has been processed.

Figure 3.8 (a) PC sending data to CPI-C and receiving an error reply

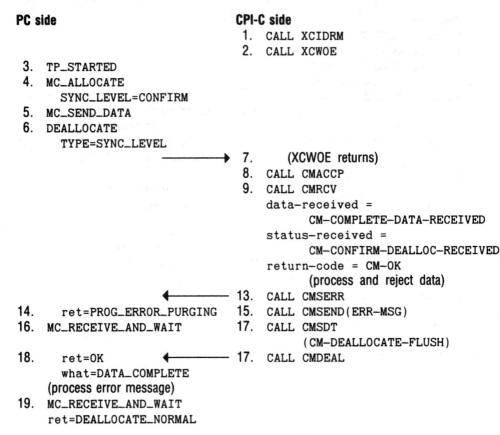

PC side

3.   TP_STARTED
4.   MC_ALLOCATE
        SYNC_LEVEL=CONFIRM
5.   MC_SEND_DATA
6.   DEALLOCATE
        TYPE=SYNC_LEVEL

14.   ret=PROG_ERROR_PURGING
16.   MC_RECEIVE_AND_WAIT

18.   ret=OK
        what=DATA_COMPLETE
      (process error message)
19.   MC_RECEIVE_AND_WAIT
        ret=DEALLOCATE_NORMAL

CPI-C side
1.   CALL XCIDRM
2.   CALL XCWOE

7.   (XCWOE returns)
8.   CALL CMACCP
9.   CALL CMRCV
        data-received =
              CM–COMPLETE–DATA–RECEIVED
        status-received =
              CM–CONFIRM–DEALLOC–RECEIVED
        return-code = CM–OK
              (process and reject data)
13.   CALL CMSERR
15.   CALL CMSEND(ERR–MSG)
17.   CALL CMSDT
        (CM–DEALLOCATE–FLUSH)
17.   CALL CMDEAL

Figure 3.8 (b) CPI-C program sending data to PC and receiving an error reply

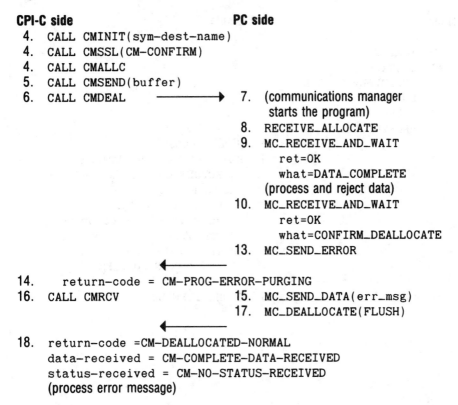

CPI-C side   **PC side**
4. CALL CMINIT(sym-dest-name)
4. CALL CMSSL(CM-CONFIRM)
4. CALL CMALLC
5. CALL CMSEND(buffer)
6. CALL CMDEAL ────────▶ 7. (communications manager
                                starts the program)
                            8. RECEIVE_ALLOCATE
                            9. MC_RECEIVE_AND_WAIT
                                  ret=OK
                                  what=DATA_COMPLETE
                                (process and reject data)
                           10. MC_RECEIVE_AND_WAIT
                                  ret=OK
                                  what=CONFIRM_DEALLOCATE
                           13. MC_SEND_ERROR
                          ◀────────
14.   return-code = CM-PROG-ERROR-PURGING
16. CALL CMRCV   15. MC_SEND_DATA(err_msg)
                      17. MC_DEALLOCATE(FLUSH)
             ◀────────
18.   return-code =CM-DEALLOCATED-NORMAL
       data-received = CM-COMPLETE-DATA-RECEIVED
       status-received = CM-NO-STATUS-RECEIVED
       (process error message)

Notes to Figures 3.8a–3.8b

13. The remote program issues an error to indicate that it does not like the data.
14. The deallocate in the local program returns with an error.
15. The remote program sends an error message to say why the data were rejected.
16. The local program issues a receive to obtain the error message.
17. The remote program deallocates the conversation unconditionally. It can now exit before the local program obtains the error message.
18. The receive in the local program returns with the error message, and in the case of the CPI-C program also the DEALLOCATION indication.
19. The PC version of the local program has to issue a second receive to obtain the DEALLOCATE indicator.

Figure 3.9 (a) PC sending data to an AS/400 program and receiving a confirmation

PC side   **AS/400 side**

```
                                    1.  OPEN ICFFILE

  2.  TP_STARTED
  3.  MC_ALLOCATE
         SYNC_LEVEL=CONFIRM
  4.  MC_SEND_DATA
  5.  MC_DEALLOCATE
         TYPE=SYNC_LEVEL
            ──────────────▶  6.  (OPEN returns)
                             8.  READ ICFFILE specifying
                                    RCVDETACH, RCVCONFIRM
                                   return-code = 001C
                                      RCVDETACH indicator set
                                      RCVCONFIRM indicator set
                                  (process data)
                            10.  WRITE ICFFILE specifying
                                             RSPCONFIRM
            ◀──────────────
 11.  ret=OK                19.  CLOSE ICFFILE
```

Figure 3.9 (b) AS/400 program sending data to PC and receiving a confirmation

AS/400 side   **PC side**
```
1.  OPEN ICFFILE
3.  WRITE ICFFILE specifying
            EVOKE
4.  WRITE ICFFILE FROM buffer
5.  WRITE ICFFILE specifying
            DETACH CONFIRM RCVFAIL
                        ─────────▶  6.  (communications manager
                                        starts the program)
                                    7.  RECEIVE_ALLOCATE
                                    8.  MC_RECEIVE_AND_WAIT
                                           ret=OK
                                           what=DATA_COMPLETE
                                        (process data)
                                    9.  MC_RECEIVE_AND_WAIT
                                           ret=OK
                                           what=CONFIRM_DEALLOCATE
                                   10.  MC_CONFIRMED
                        ◀─────────
11.     return-code = 0000
19.  CLOSE ICFFILE
```

Notes to Figures 3.9a–3.9b

1. The first action of an AS/400 program using APPC is to open the ICF file. This must be done by the receiving program so that it can accept incoming allocates.
2. The local PC program must identify itself to the communications manager.
3. Allocate the conversation.
4. Send the data.
5. Conditionally deallocate the conversation.
6. The remote program starts, or returns from the acquire.
7. The remote PC program issues a RECEIVE ALLOCATE to pick up the conversation.
8. The remote program receives the data. The AS/400 program also receives the CONDITIONAL DEALLOCATE indicators.
9. The remote PC program has to issue a second receive to obtain the CONDITIONAL DEALLOCATE status return.
10. The remote program issues a confirmation to indicate that it has successfully processed the data.
11. The deallocate in the local program returns OK. The local program now knows that the data has been processed.
19. The AS/400 programs have to clean up by closing the ICF file or issuing an EOS.

Figure 3.10 (a) PC sending data to AS/400 and receiving an error reply

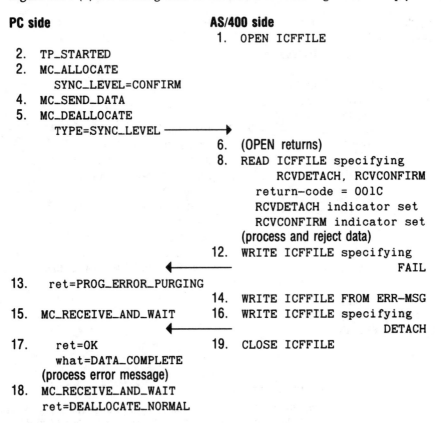

PC side	**AS/400 side**
	1. OPEN ICFFILE
2. TP_STARTED	
2. MC_ALLOCATE	
SYNC_LEVEL=CONFIRM	
4. MC_SEND_DATA	
5. MC_DEALLOCATE	
TYPE=SYNC_LEVEL ⟶	
	6. (OPEN returns)
	8. READ ICFFILE specifying
	RCVDETACH, RCVCONFIRM
	return–code = 001C
	RCVDETACH indicator set
	RCVCONFIRM indicator set
	(process and reject data)
	12. WRITE ICFFILE specifying
⟵	FAIL
13. ret=PROG_ERROR_PURGING	
	14. WRITE ICFFILE FROM ERR–MSG
15. MC_RECEIVE_AND_WAIT	16. WRITE ICFFILE specifying
⟵	DETACH
17. ret=OK	19. CLOSE ICFFILE
what=DATA_COMPLETE	
(process error message)	
18. MC_RECEIVE_AND_WAIT	
ret=DEALLOCATE_NORMAL	

Figure 3.10 (b) AS/400 sending data to PC and receiving an error reply

AS/400 side   **PC side**
```
1.  OPEN ICFFILE
3.  WRITE ICFFILE specifying
              EVOKE
4.  WRITE ICFFILE FROM buffer
5.  WRITE ICFFILE specifying
       DETACH CONFIRM RCVFAIL
              ─────────────────────►  6.  (communications manager
                                           starts the program)
                                       7.  RECEIVE_ALLOCATE
                                       8.  MC_RECEIVE_AND_WAIT
                                              ret=OK
                                              what=DATA_COMPLETE
                                           (process and reject data)
                                       9.  MC_RECEIVE_AND_WAIT
                                              ret=OK
                                              what=CONFIRM_DEALLOCATE
                                      12.  MC_SEND_ERROR
              ◄─────────────────────
13.  return-code = 83C9
       RCVFAIL indicator set           14.  MC_SEND_DATA(err_msg)
15.  READ ICFFILE specifying
              RCVDETACH
                                      16.  MC_DEALLOCATE(FLUSH)
              ◄─────────────────────
17.    return-code = 0008
         RCVDETACH indicator set
     (process error message)
19.  CLOSE ICFFILE
```

Notes to Figures 3.10a–3.10b

12. The remote program issues an error to indicate that it does not like the data.
13. The deallocate in the local program returns with an error.
14. The remote program sends an error message to say why the data were rejected.
15. The local program issues a receive to obtain the error message.
16. The remote program deallocates the conversation. It can now exit even before the local program receives the error message.
17. The receive in the local program returns with the error message, and in the case of the AS/400 program also the DEALLOCATION indication.
18. The PC version of the local program has to issue a second receive to obtain the DEALLOCATE indicator.

SUMMARY

We have now covered all the main features of APPC as implemented in four different environments. This is sufficient to write applications providing the bridge between IBM mainframe and midrange computers and PCs. This can form the basis of SAA-compliant cooperative processing systems.

There are a few more items to cover, such as security features, without which you will not be able to access mainframe transactions, and some system-dependent features, such as how TPs are started and how to optimize them. These topics are covered in the next chapter.

4 Advanced APPC Programming

4.1 INTRODUCTION

This chapter covers the remaining features of APPC, namely security and basic conversations, and looks at some of the peculiarities of each of the systems separately. These include:

- The program startup options under OS/2 and on CMS with AVS.
- The sync-point features of CICS.
- Use of the presentation manager with APPC programs under OS/2.
- The APPC subset implemented by the IMS APPC bridge product.

No attempt is made to describe these system-dependent features in terms of other systems: they are *too* system dependent.

Most of the information in this chapter will not be needed for most applications. For instance, in the typical case of a system where PCs provide a front end for CICS transactions, there is no need to know about program startup on PCs, sync-pointing under CICS, or the IMS bridge, while basic conversations are generally best avoided.

4.2 BASIC CONVERSATIONS

There is another set of APPC verbs which give access at a slightly lower level to the LU 6.2 facilities. The main difference between the mapped and the basic, or unmapped, facilities is that in a mapped conversation each SEND causes a single message to be sent. In a basic conversation the objects sent are GDS (generalized data stream) **variables**. The messages in a mapped conversation are mapped into GDS variables.

A GDS variable consists of a two-byte length field, followed by a two-byte id field, followed by data. The length field is encoded in the normal fashion for the mainframe, i.e. high-order byte first, the other way round from the normal way for a PC (see Fig. 4.1).

Figure 4.1 A generalized data stream

L L	I D	data . . .

1 2 3 4 5 . . .

The difference between mapped and basic conversations really only affects the behaviour of the SEND and RECEIVE verbs. For a basic conversation, the data to be transferred are a sequence of GDS variables. These may be concatenated and sent by one verb, or broken down into several buffers and sent using several SENDs. It does not make any difference to the actual information transmitted how the data is passed to SEND: only the GDS headers affect it. Thus, for example, three GDS strings can be sent in two calls when the data is arranged in the buffers as shown in Fig 4.2.

Figure 4.2 Sending three GDS strings in two cells

SEND length=25

0008	I D	data	000D	I D	more data	0011	I D

     1 – 8   9 – 21   22 – 25

SEND length = 13

yet more data

   1 – 13

In the first call 25 bytes are sent, and in the second call 13 bytes are sent. This results in three GDSs being sent. When a partial GDS has been passed to APPC, the conversation is in an odd state where the GDS must be completed or abandoned. Thus PREPARE–TO–RECEIVE, for example, cannot be issued, only another SEND_DATA or a SEND_ERROR (or ISSUE ERROR) or a DEALLOCATE ABEND (ISSUE ABEND).

RECEIVE too behaves in a different way. There is an additional parameter which indicates whether APPC is to divide the data into GDSs for the program, or whether the buffer should simply be filled.

There is an additional return code that many verbs can return: PROG_ERROR_TRUNC. This indicates that the remote program issued a SEND_ERROR in the middle of sending a GDS.

OS/2

On the PC the verbs are very similar to their mapped equivalents: only one field in the control block indicates whether the verb is the mapped or basic variety.

The OS/2 communications manager verbs RECEIVE_AND_WAIT, RECEIVE_IMMEDIATE, and SEND_DATA are very similar to their mapped equivalents. The receive verbs use an additional field called fill which can take the values BUFFER or LL. These are equivalent to the CICS GDS RECEIVE options BUFFER and LLID.

The verbs DEALLOCATE and SEND_ERROR have a pair of additional parameters: LOG_DATA and LOG_DATA_LENGTH. For DEALLOCATE these should be NULL and 0 respectively, except when deallocate_type is ABEND when log data may be specified. Log data is not passed to the partner TP but may be logged; it will appear in buffer traces and may help in diagnosing problems.

The data pointed to by the LOG_DATA parameter must be a GDS string, the length field must be the same as the LOG_DATA_LENGTH parameter, and must have the structure shown in Fig. 4.3.

Figure 4.3 LOG_DATA structure

LL	12E1	PSlen	PSid	MsgLen	message

LL, PSlen and MsgLen are two-byte integers, high-order byte first. PSid is a 'product set vector', and can be omitted, in which case PSlen is 2, as the lengths given always include the length field. The message should be in EBCDIC. The format of the product set vector is given in IBM's *Systems Network Architecture Formats Manual* GA27–3136–10.

CICS

The CICS commands are substantially different from their mapped equivalents, and cannot be used in COBOL, only assembler. The CICS verbs are all of the form:

```
EXEC CICS GDS . . .
```

To interpret the GDS commands the assembler XOPT(GDS) parameter is required by the CICS translator. The command that follows the word GDS is very similar to the mapped commands, with the exception of the SEND and RECEIVE commands. The biggest difference is in the way that the conversation id and status data are handled. The GDS commands do not use the EIB. Most verbs, with the exception of GDS ALLOCATE and GDS EXTRACT PROCESS take two additional parameters, CONVDATA and RETCODE. CONVDATA is a structure 24 bytes long that contains the status variables for the conversation. Its structure is as follows:

```
CDBCOMPL DS   C      X'FF' => data complete
CDBSYNC  DS   C      X'FF' => SYNCPOINT required
CDBFREE  DS   C      X'FF' => FREE required
CDBRECV  DS   C      X'FF' => RECEIVE required
CDBSIG   DS   C      X'FF' => SIGNAL received
CDBCONF  DS   C      X'FF' => CONFIRM received
CDBERR   DS   C      X'FF' => ERROR received
CDBERRCD DS   CL4    error code if CDBERR set
CDBSYNRB DS   C      X'FF' => ROLLBACK required
CDBRSVD  DS   CL12   reserved
```

RETCODE specifies a six-byte storage area that gives details of errors that prevented execution of the verb, such as resource failure or a verb being issued when the conversation is in an unsuitable state.

The GDS ALLOCATE command also takes the additional parameter CONVID. This must specify a four-byte storage area for the returned conversation id. The GDS SEND command has the following form:

```
EXEC CICS GDS SEND                                        *
                [FROM(buffer) FLENGTH(length)]  *
                [INVITE | LAST]                           *
                [CONFIRM | WAIT]                           *
                CONVID(conv-id)                           *
                CONVDATA(conv-data)                        *
                RETCODE(ret-code)
```

The effect of the INVITE, LAST, CONFIRM and WAIT options are exactly the same as for mapped conversations.

The form of the GDS RECEIVE command is as follows:

```
EXEC CICS GDS RECEIVE                                     *
                {INTO(buffer) | SET(pointer-ret)} *
                FLENGTH(length-returned)                  *
                MAXFLENGTH(size-of-buffer)     *
                {BUFFER | LLID}                           *
                CONVID(conv-id)                           *
                CONVDATA(conv-data)                        *
                RETCODE(ret-code)
```

If you specify the option BUFFER, then the receive will not return until either MAXFLENGTH bytes have been received, or the remote transaction has finished sending. If you specify LLID, then receive will return as soon as it either has finished receiving a GDS, or has received MAX-FLENGTH. If the original GDS exceeds the size of the buffer then a partial GDS will be returned, and CDBCOMPL will not be set, indicating that the data is incomplete. Subsequent RECEIVEs will return the rest of the GDS. Once the remainder of the GDS has been returned, CDBCOMPL will be set. The meaning of the other CONVDATA fields are the same as the mapped EIB variables.

CPI-C

CPI-C does not have any additional verbs. The only difference between the use of mapped and basic conversations is that the characteristic conversation–type has to be set to CM–BASIC–CONVERSATION by calling the function CMSCT. The choice between receiving GDS strings or undecoded buffers is achieved by setting the characteristic fill. This is set using the function call CMSF to either CM–FILL–LL or CM–FILL–BUFFER.

AS/400

On the AS/400 you differentiate between a mapped and a basic conversation by an attribute you set on the ICF file. Thus for a basic conversation you need the command

```
OVRICFDEVE PGMDEV(pgndev) RMTLOCNAME(loc)
CNVTYPE(*USER)
```

The cnvtype defaults to *SYSTEM which gives you a mapped conversation. There is no equivalent to the fill command on the receive command: you always have GDS strings passed back.

4.3 APPC SECURITY

There are two types of security defined for APPC. These are **session-level** (or **LU–LU**) **security**, and **conversation-level security**. In session-level security the acceptance or rejection of the password is done when the session is established between the two LUs. In conversation-level security a user id and password is given by the program attempting to start a conversation; this combination is verified at the receiving end before the TP is started. The TP at the receiving end can extract the user id given, but it is not given the password. It is possible to ask the system to fill in the user id by specifying SECURITY(SAME) on an allocate. This means that a program can pass on to another system a request with user id without having to know the password. The user id is passed on without a password, but with the *already-verified* flag set. Systems can be configured to accept or reject already-verified user ids.

For session-level security the password is never actually sent to the destination computer. What happens is that the destination computer sends some random data back as part of the session startup. This is encrypted using the password, sent back, and then compared to the same data encrypted using the password associated with the session on the destination computer. For conversation-level security the user id and password are sent from one machine to the other.

OS/2

Session-level security is set up by selecting 'Yes' for LU–LU session security on the create/change partner LU profile. This causes another panel to be presented asking for the password.

Conversation-level security is set up by selecting 'Yes' for conversation security on the create/change partner LU profile and by specifying a security type of AP_PGM and the user id and password in the ALLOCATE verb, or by specifying a security type of AP_SAME. To accept incoming conversations using conversation security, the valid user id and password pairs must be configured into the communications manager using the conversation security profiles menus. The user id is passed to the receiving program in the RECEIVE_ALLOCATE verb. An ALLO–CATE attempt that is rejected because the user id or password is wrong returns with return_code set to AP_PARAMETER_CHECK and the secondary re-turn_code set to AP_BAD_SECURITY. Remember that the user id and password have to be specified in EBCDIC. An incoming allocate with security specified as none, and therefore with no user id or password, will still be accepted by the communications manager even if conversation-level security is configured as 'yes'. However, such an incoming allocate will be presented to the program through RE–CEIVE_ALLOCATE as having security type AP_NONE and with no user id. In this case it is up to the TP to take appropriate action, such as abending the conversation and logging the attempt as a security violation.

CICS

Session-level security is set up by specifying the BINDPWD = PASSWORD option on the DFHTCT command for the terminal definition for the remote LU.

Conversation-level security for incoming allocates is an attribute of each TP, and is set up in exactly the same way as for 3270 sessions. The only security type available for outbound allocates is SECURITY(SAME), so the current user id and password are used for outbound allocates.

CPI-C

For outbound conversations, conversation-level security is invoked by specifying the conversation security type to XC-SECURITY-PROGRAM using the function XCSCST, and by specifying a conversation security user id and password using the functions XCSCSU and XCSCSP.

For incoming allocates, security is checked at several levels. First, if a user id and password are specified in the allocate then they must be valid for the system: VM checks the user id. If the allocate is for a private resource then the user id must either be in the $SERVER$ NAME entry for the resource, or be the same as the user id given for the gateway if the gateway is dedicated.

Incoming allocates with security type NONE are only accepted by global resources or by private resources accessed through dedicated gateways and which specify * as their access list in $SERVER$ NAMES.

AS/400

For outbound conversations, conversation-level security is specified by including the keyword SECURITY in the format along with the keyword EVOKE. The format of the SECURITY keyword is:

SECURITY(1 profile-id)

or

SECURITY(3 user-id 2 password)

Profile id can be either *USER indicating that the current user's profile should be used, or *NONE implying that no user id or password should be sent. This is equivalent to not specifying SECURITY at all. USER—ID and pass—word may be either literal values enclosed in single quotes ('), or field names. For instance:

                    SECURITY (3 'USER43' 2 &PWD)
    PWD 10A

At the receiving end the AS/400 looks for a user profile to match the user id and password if they are specified in the incoming allocate. If no user id and password were sent in the allocate, then the default user id is used. This is the user id given in the DFTUSR parameter of the ADDCMNE command. If the user profile thus selected does not have the authority to run the program specified in the allocate then the allocate is rejected with a security violation.

4.4 CONSIDER-ATIONS FOR PROGRAMMING OS/2

The way programs start as a result of incoming allocates depends on how the TP is configured in the communications manager. There are three types of TP operation:

4.4.1 Receive_allocate *and CM TP configuration*

1 Queued – attach manager started.
2 Queued – operator started.
3 Non-queued – attach manager started.

If a TP is defined as non-queued, then as soon as the incoming allocate arrives, the attach manager, which is part of the communications manager, starts the program which should immediately issue a RECEIVE_ALLOCATE to accept the allocate. When the conversation has terminated the program should either exit or at least issue the verb TP_ended. This is the configuration most akin to the behaviour of TPs under CICS.

If a TP is defined as 'queued – attach manager started' then an incoming allocate causes the program to be started *only if there is no TP of that name already running.* If there is such a TP already running, using a different LU or another session in a parallel session group, then the incoming allocate is held in a queue for a time until the old

TP either exits or issues a RECEIVE_ALLOCATE. The length of time an allocate is queued before being rejected is configurable.

The intention here is that the incoming allocate starts the program. When the program has finished a conversation, it issues another RECEIVE_ALLOCATE to pick up the next incoming allocate. This enables conversations to be accepted much faster, as it eliminates the time it takes to load the program off disk. However, it does mean that incoming allocates are serialized. If conversations are short-lived, this does not matter, but queued TP operation may be inappropriate for long-lived TPs.

It is worth noting that while only one program can issue a RECEIVE_ALLOCATE of a queued operation TP, that program can handle several conversations at the same time. It can, for instance, start a new thread for each conversation as soon as RECEIVE_ALLOCATE returns, then immediately reissue the RECEIVE_ALLOCATE.

If the program issues a RECEIVE_ALLOCATE and there is no incoming allocate queued then the RECEIVE_ALLOCATE is held for a period of time in case an allocate arrives. If no allocate arrives in time then the RECEIVE_ALLOCATE returns with return—code AP_UNSUCCESSFUL. The period of time the system allows RECEIVE_ALLOCATE to wait can be configured to be between 0 and 480 minutes.

The behaviour of operator-started TPs is very similar to 'queued – attach manager started' except that if the program is not running then, rather than the program being started, a message is presented to the operator to start the program.

The difference between queued and non-queued TP operation obviously affects the structure of the program, but the difference is limited to the beginning and end of the program. A non-queued program is simpler, starting with a RECEIVE_ALLOCATE and ending with a TP_ENDED after which the program exits. A queued program is likely to have a loop which contains much the same code as a non-queued program, but looping back from the TP_ENDED to the RECEIVE_ALLOCATE, and exiting only if the RECEIVE_ALLOCATE fails.

4.4.2 APPC and presentation manager programs

The presentation manager under OS/2 is the driving force that makes the use of PCs as programmable workstations attached to mainframes attractive. Programming for the presentation manager is, however, rather different from programming more conventional application programs, and this is not the place to discuss how to write presentation manager programs.

There are, however, several points that apply especially to programs that use communications. Time-consuming operations, such as communicating with a mainframe TP, must take place in a separate thread from the one controlling the windows. This is mandatory, otherwise the user can be locked out from the system, unable to interact with other tasks on the 'desk top' until the functions complete.

The sample code given for the PC in Appendix A shows a typical small presentation manager program. In it a thread is started which introduces itself to the communications manager and then waits for commands from the other thread. These commands take the form of a record containing data and a command word. When a command is ready, the foreground thread puts up a message asking the user to wait, disables the functions that use APPC and clears a semaphore to allow the APPC thread to process the command. When the APPC thread has finished processing the request (successfully or not), it posts a message to the foreground thread which re-enables the functions previously disabled, removes the wait message and displays the received data.

It is perfectly reasonable for the user to continue with local processing while awaiting a reply from the mainframe transaction. This could involve other APPC conversations, but not using the same thread. You would want one thread per conversation.

4.5 CONSIDERATIONS FOR APPC USE WITH CICS

CICS contains the concept of transaction rollback, whereby all the actions carried out by a transaction since the last syncpoint are undone. APPC, as defined for CICS, contains special features to enable syncpointing and rolling back to be propagated amongst a set of cooperating transaction programs. The OS/2, CPI-C and AS/400 implementations do not support the syncpoint features, and so have to be dealt with using the confirm/confirmed handshaking.

The CICS SYNCPOINT command affects LU 6.2 conversations, or at least those allocated with SYNCLEVEL(2). For a SYNCPOINT command to be allowed, all SYNC-LEVEL(2) conversations that the TP is using must be in send state for that transaction. The SYNCPOINT command causes the RECEIVEs issued by the remote TPs to return with EIBSYNC set.

When a TP receives a syncpoint notification it has a limited choice of actions. The two preferred options are to issue a SYNCPOINT or SYNCPOINT ROLLBACK command, thus allowing the syncpointing process to continue or to cause it to fail and roll back. The other options are to issue one of the commands ISSUE ERROR or ISSUE ABEND.

Issuing an error indication causes the other TPs involved in the syncpointing to abend. The program issuing the error is not abended, but must issue a RECEIVE which returns with EIBSYNRB and the TP must then issue a SYNCPOINT ROLLBACK.

ISSUE ABEND causes all TPs involved in the syncpointing to abend, and should not be used by programs that have modified any recoverable resources.

If a syncpoint is started and one of the TPs involved issues a SYNCPOINT ROLLBACK then the other TPs are notified of this in one of two ways. If a program has already been notified that a syncpoint is under way, and has issued a SYNCPOINT, then it returns with EIBRLDBK set and the recoverable resources are rolled back. If it has not yet been notified of the syncpointing then its outstanding RECEIVE returns with EIBSYNRB set and it must then issue a SYNCPOINT ROLLBACK.

There is another command associated with syncpointing, and that is ISSUE PREPARE. This command is issued to particular TPs before issuing a general SYNCPOINT. This allows some control over the order in which syncpointing is done. The effect of issuing an ISSUE PREPARE is to go through the first part of the syncpoint interchange with a TP. This leaves that TP with a SYNCPOINT pending. It is important that once a TP has issued an

ISSUE PREPARE to another TP it eventually issues a SYNCPOINT.

If there are conversations active which were not allocated with SYNCLEVEL(2), such as conversations to PCs, and if the programs at the far end control recoverable resources such as databases, then you may want to emulate the syncpointing for those conversations. This can be done by defining suitable higher level protocol, but generally you should make do with the confirm/confirmed handshaking.

Figs. 4.4–4.6 show examples of syncpoint processing.

Figure 4.4 Normal CICS syncpoint processing

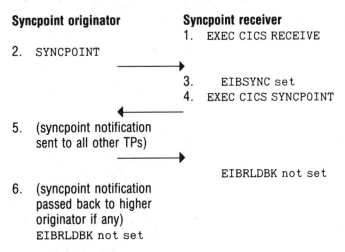

Syncpoint originator

2. SYNCPOINT

5. (syncpoint notification
    sent to all other TPs)

6. (syncpoint notification
    passed back to higher
    originator if any)
    EIBRLDBK not set

Syncpoint receiver

1. EXEC CICS RECEIVE

3.   EIBSYNC set
4.   EXEC CICS SYNCPOINT

EIBRLDBK not set

Notes to Figure 4.4

1. Before a program can issue a SYNCPOINT it has to be in send state for all SYNCLEVEL(2) conversations. Therefore all syncpoint receivers must have issued RECEIVEs.
2. Originator issues a SYNCPOINT. This might be in response to a syncpoint request received from another TP.
3. The receive returns with a syncpoint indicator.
4. The receiver then issues a SYNCPOINT. This might make it the originator of a syncpoint request on other conversations.
5. The originator continues to issue syncpoint notifications to other TPs. When all transaction programs have issued SYNCPOINT commands then the originator goes back to each TP in turn and allows their SYNCPOINTs to complete.
6. When all lower TPs have completed syncpoint processing, the higher TP may proceed as a syncpoint receiver from just after state 4.

Figure 4.5 Syncpoint backout processing (1)

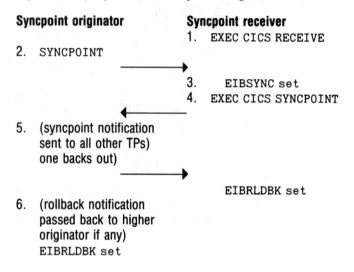

Syncpoint originator	Syncpoint receiver

Notes to Figure 4.5

1. Before a program can issue a SYNCPOINT it has to be in send state for all SYNCLEVEL(2) conversations. Therefore all syncpoint receivers must have issued RECEIVEs.
2. Originator issues a SYNCPOINT. This might be in response to a syncpoint request received from another TP.
3. The receive returns with a syncpoint indicator.
4. The receiver then issues a SYNCPOINT. This might make it the originator of a syncpoint request on other conversations.
5. The originator continues to issue syncpoint notifications to other TPs. When all TPs have issued SYNCPOINT or SYNCPOINT ROLLBACK commands then the originator goes back to each TP in turn and allows their SYNCPOINTs or SYNCPOINT ROLLBACKs to complete.
6. When all lower TPs have completed rolling back, the higher TP may proceed as a syncpoint receiver from just after state 4.

Figure 4.6 Syncpoint backout processing (2)

Syncpoint originator	Syncpoint receiver
	1. EXEC CICS RECEIVE
2. SYNCPOINT	
3. (syncpoint notification sent to some other TPs) one backs out)	
⟶	
	4. EIBSYNRB set
	5. EXEC CICS SYNCPOINT ROLLBACK
⟵	
6. (rollback notification sent to all previous TPs. as in the previous figure backout notification sent to all remaining TPs)	
7. (rollback notification passed back to higher originator if any) EIBRLDBK set	

Notes to Figure 4.6

1. Before a program can issue a SYNCPOINT it has to be in send state for all SYNCLEVEL(2) conversations. Therefore all syncpoint receivers must have issued RECEIVEs.
2. Originator issues a SYNCPOINT. This might be in response to a syncpoint request received from another TP.
3. Another TP, which received a syncpoint notification before this one, backed out, causing the syncpoint to fail.
4. The receive returns with a syncpoint backout indicator.
5. The receiver then issues a SYNCPOINT ROLLBACK. This might make it the originator of a syncpoint rollback request on other conversations.
6. The originator continues to issue syncpoint backout notifications to other TPs.
7. When all lower TPs have completed rolling back, the higher TP may proceed as a syncpoint receiver from just after state 5.

4.6 CONSIDERA-TIONS FOR CPI-C/CMS

The way a CMS program uses the commands XCIDRM, XCWOE, XCTRRM and CMACCP depends on how the resource is configured and on the parameters passed to XCIDRM. If the resource is a global resource then the program has to be running before the incoming allocate arrives. Otherwise the resource is not defined, and the allocate is rejected. A typical program managing a global resource issues the call XCIDRM to define the resource as its first action, and defines it with service mode XC-SEQUENTIAL. The program then loops as shown:

```
        CALL "XCIDRM" USING RESOURCE-NAME
                            XC-GLOBAL
                            XC-SEQUENTIAL
                            XC-REJECT-SECURITY-NONE
                            RETURN-CODE.
MAIN-LOOP.
        CALL "XCWOE" USING  RESOURCE-NAME
                            CONVERSATION-ID
                            EVENT-TYPE
                            DATA-LENGTH
                            CONSOLE-INPUT-BUFFER
                            RETURN-CODE.
    IF EVENT-TYPE NOT = XC-ALLOCATION-REQUEST
        CALL "XCTRRM" USING RESOURCE-NAME
                            RETURN CODE
        STOP RUN.
    PERFORM CONVERSATION THROUGH END-CONVERSATION.
    GO TO MAIN-LOOP.
```

This would also be an appropriate structure for a program controlling a private resource accessed through a dedicated gateway. For a private resource accessed through a non-dedicated gateway you would want a much simpler program. In this case, the program would be started as a result of the incoming allocate, and need not call XCIDRM, XCWOE, or XCTRRM. The first call would be CMACCP, and the last CMDEAL.

4.7 IMS AND APPC

IMS does not support APPC until IMS v3.2. There is, however, an APPC mechanism for submitting transactions into an IMS queue. This is rather limited and only certain actions are allowed. For instance, the APPC program connected to IMS is not allowed to issue the verbs SEND_ERROR, CONFIRM, or DEALLOCATE ABEND. The normal data flow is shown in Fig. 4.7.

Figure 4.7 Normal data flow with IMS bridge

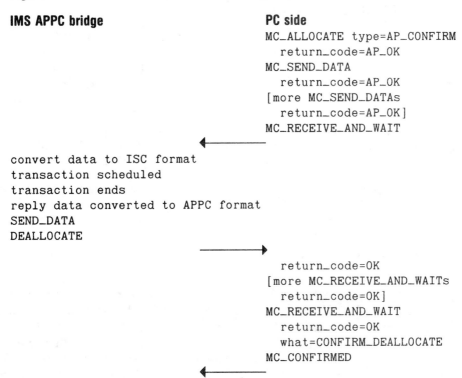

```
IMS APPC bridge                              PC side
                                   MC_ALLOCATE type=AP_CONFIRM
                                      return_code=AP_OK
                                   MC_SEND_DATA
                                      return_code=AP_OK
                                   [more MC_SEND_DATAs
                                      return_code=AP_OK]
                                   MC_RECEIVE_AND_WAIT

convert data to ISC format
transaction scheduled
transaction ends
reply data converted to APPC format
SEND_DATA
DEALLOCATE

                                      return_code=OK
                                   [more MC_RECEIVE_AND_WAITs
                                      return_code=OK]
                                   MC_RECEIVE_AND_WAIT
                                      return_code=OK
                                      what=CONFIRM_DEALLOCATE
                                   MC_CONFIRMED

output dequeued
```

The APPC bridge accepts allocates for any TP name, but if the program is unavailable then the bridge issues a SEND_ERROR followed by a SEND_DATA to send an error message back to the requesting program.

If a conversation is terminated before the reply from IMS has been received and confirmed then the data remains queued. Data that is left in the terminal queue after the conversation has ended is sent by IMS to the TP to the PC called IMSASYNC. This program has to exist to empty the queue, otherwise all subsequent attempts to send data to IMS would be rejected. The data flow to IMSASYNC is as shown in Fig. 4.8.

Figure 4.8 IMSASYNC data flow

IMS APPC bridge   **PC side**
```
MC_ALLOCATE type=CONFIRM, tpn=IMSASYNC
MC_SEND_DATA
[MC_SEND_DATA]
MC_DEALLOCATE type=SYNC_LEVEL
                                    ────────────────▶
                                    RECEIVE_ALLOCATE
                                        return_code=AP_OK
                                    MC_RECEIVE_AND_WAIT
                                        return_code=OK
                                        what=AP_DATA_COMPLETE
                                    [MC_RECEIVE_AND_WAIT
                                        return_code=OK
                                        what=AP_DATA_COMPLETE]
                                    MC_RECEIVE_AND_WAIT
                                        return_code=
                                            AP_CONFIRM_DEALLOCATE
                                    MC_CONFIRMED
                                        return_code=AP_OK
                                    ◀────────────────
output dequeued
```

It is possible to arrange for all responses to come from IMS via the IMSASYNC TP. This is done by issuing a DEALLOCATE immediately after sending the data.

Attention must be paid to the problems that may occur if the link fails. There are two possibilities. First, the link may fail between the time the PC issues the RECEIVE AND WAIT or DEALLOCATE and the time that a response is received. Was the transaction queued? The PC cannot tell. If it is important that the transaction is not run twice, then the best solution is to put sequence numbers in the requests.

Ambiguity also arises if the link fails between the time the adapter issues its DEALLOCATE and the time it receives a response. Did the PC receive the reply? The adapter cannot tell, so it assumes that it did not, and the reply remains queued. The adapter sends the data again. Thus the PC program must be able to identify duplicate data and act accordingly.

The IMS program knows nothing about APPC. It still

reads data off the queue using Get Unique (GU) and Get Next (GN), and replying using Insert (ISRT). The only changes that may have to be made to existing 3270-style IMS programs are related to sequence-numbering requests and replies, and the removal of any message format service (MFS) dependencies. The removal of message formats lifts a load from IMS, and means that the records received by the PC are the same as those handled by the IMS TP.

REFERENCES FOR APPC PROGRAMMING

IBM Operating System/2 Extended Edition Version 1.3 APPC Programmers Reference, IBM Corporation, Boca Raton FL, January 1991.

Customer Information Control System/DOS/VS Version 1.7 Intercommunication Facilities Guide, IBM Corporation, Mechanicsburgh, PA, July 1987.

Systems Application Architecture Common Programming Interface, Communications Reference, IBM Corporation, Armonk, NY, October 1988.

AS/400 Communications: Programmers Guide, IBM Corporation, Rochester, NY, September 1990.

AS/400 Communications: Advanced Program–to–Program Communications and Advanced Peer–to–Peer Networking User's Guide, IBM Corporation, Rochester, NY, September 1989.

IBM Systems Network Architecture: Formats, IBM Corporation, Research Triangle Park, NC, June 1991.

5 Configuring APPC

5.1 INTRODUCTION One of the unfortunate facts of life is that before two machines can communicate they have to be told about each other. When attaching a PC through an SNA network to CICS this means configuring the PC (the communications manager under OS/2), VTAM and CICS.

VTAM (virtual telecommunications access method) and NCP (network control program for a 3725 or 3745) between them control all communications between a 370 or 390 mainframe computer and all other SNA (and some non-SNA) devices and computers. The scope of this book does not allow a complete description of VTAM and NCP, so to simplify things, and to give a flavour of the configuration details required in a mainframe, I have considered the case where an FEP (front-end processor or 37x5) is inappropriate, that is, the case where the mainframe's communications hardware is under VTAM's control. Generically, the communications hardware is known as an integral channel adapter (ICA).

To the uninitiated, configuring VTAM seems like a black art. Most configurations are used because they work and changes are only made when they have to be. The situation is not improved by having part of the definition for LU 6.2 terminals in VTAM and part in CICS.

To establish the connection in VTAM, you have to specify: the definition of the LINE to be used; the PU definition of the PC to be attached; the LUs in the PC; and the LOGMODE or LOGMODEs to be used. Obviously the PU and LU for the mainframe and CICS also need to be defined, but these will typically already exist. The VTAM definitions must match the definitions given in the OS/2 communications manager.

Some of the VTAM parameters are for optimizing the performance of the SNA network and do not affect the configuration of the PC, but the rest have to match. To make life more difficult, the names of almost all the parameters are different on the PC from those on VTAM. By and large, VTAM configuration should only be attempted with the help of an experienced network systems programmer.

5.2 VTAM DEFINITION

VTAM definitions are hierarchical, reflecting the structure of an SNA network as seen from the mainframe. There are **groups**, lines, PUs and LUs. A group is a collection of lines with similar characteristics. Within these groups there are the individual lines. Accessed off each of these lines there may be several PUs, then within each of these PUs there will be several LUs.

Thus there are GROUP definition statements which control the subsequent LINE definition statements, which control the following PU statements, which in turn control the following LU statements. There will also be lists of PUs which may not always be connected: those PUs that are dial-up or which are token-ring attached.

The logical connections between LUs (sessions) do not follow this hierarchy, and are handled by having references from one LU to another. This is the LOGAPPL keyword in the LU definition.

The GROUP statement specifies that all the lines defined within the group are synchronous data link control (SDLC) lines. Your existing VTAM definitions will already contain such a statement. Any SDLC lines you need for LU 6.2 connection will go within such an existing GROUP:

```
SDLC034 GROUP LNCTL=SDLC
```

The LINE statement defines the characteristics of the line to be used to connect to the PU:

```
DGA034LL LINE ADDRESS=034,REPLYTO=5.0,SERVLIM=255
```

The PU statement contains the definition of the PC's PU. This contains several parameters that have to match the definitions on the PC. The parameters that must match are the ADDR, which in the communications manager is called 'link station address', MAXDATA which must be nine greater than the maximum RU size specified in the communications manager, and MAXOUT which is called 'send window count'.

```
DGAPUL PU ADDR=Cl,SSCPFM=USSSCS,MAXDATA=265,          X
          MAXOUT=7,PASSLIM=7,                         X
          VPACING=7,PACING=7,                         X
          DISCNT=(NO,F)
```

For a switched connection which includes token-ring, there will be IDBLK and IDNUM parameters:

```
IDBLK=05D,IDNUM=78764
```

The IDNUM parameters must match the XID specified on the PC. The PC name does not actually have to match, but should to avoid confusion.

The LU statements define the LUs on the PC. This too contains parameters that must match the definition in the PC. These are the name, the LOCADDR, which is called the LU local address (NAU address), and the DLOGMOD, which must be defined as the mode for the partner LU:

```
DGAALO1 LU LOCADDR=7,SSCPFM=FSS,             X
           LOGAPPL=DGACICS                   X
           DLOGMOD=LU62,MODETAB=DGAMODE
```

The MODEENT statements define the mode (class of service) to be used for the connection. The parameters that must match are the name, PSNDPAC and the RUSIZES. PSNDPAC needs to match the receive pacing limit in the mode entry in the communication manager configuration. The RUSIZES are encoded as a 4-byte hexadecimal field in VTAM as X'abcd', representing the maximum request unit (RU) sizes that may be sent by the primary and secondary LUs. These maxima are a * 2**b for the secondary LU and c * 2**d for the primary LU, where a and c can take values 8 to F, and b and d can take values between 0 and F. On the PC you specify the maximum and minimum RU sizes as actual sizes. To match, therefore, the maximum RU sizes have to be the same for both the primary and secondary LU, and the maximum and minimum sizes have to be the same. Thus if in VTAM you have

```
RUSIZES=X'8585'
```

then on the PC you must have

```
Minimum RU size . . . [256]
Maximum RU size . . . [256]
```

A LOCADDR value of zero is a special case, and implies that the LU is an **independent LU**. Independent LUs were not supported by VTAM until relatively recently, but are required if parallel or multiple sessions are to be used.

A typical MODEENT statement in the VTAM tables would look like:

```
LU62 MODEENT LOGMODE=LU62,TYPE=0,                              X
        FMPROF=X'13',TSPROF=X'07',                             X
        PRIPROT=X'B0',SECPROT=X'B0',COMPROT=X'50B1',           X
        SSNDPAC=X'00',SRCVPAC=X'00',PSNDPAC=X'05',             X
        RUSIZES=X'8585',                                       X
        PSERVIC=X'0602000000000000000002C00'
```

Note that if you are using VTAM with AVS and CMS then the last four characters of PSERVIC should be 2F00. This sets up a group of parallel sessions between the two LUs instead of one single session.

For dial-up PUs and token-ring- attached PUs, the definitions appear in a list preceded by a VBUILD TYPE=SWLIST statement. For token-ring PUs, their definition may include a MACADDR clause which contains the token-ring address of the PU.

5.3 CICS TABLE ENTRIES

There are four CICS tables that may need either adjustment or new entries for use with LU 6.2. These are the **system initialization table** (DFHSIT), the **terminal control table** (DFHTCT), the **processing program table** (DFHPPT) and **program control table** (DFHPCT). Before a TP can use the APPC, the intersystem communications must be included in CICS by specifying ISC=YES on the DFHSIT macro:

```
DFHSIT EXEC=YES,ISC=YES
```

The terminal control table completes the LU 6.2 definition of the remote PC. CICS considers all remote LUs to be terminals. So remote computers with which it is to communicate are defined as terminals of type SYSTEM. A typical TCT entry would be:

```
DFHTCT TYPE=SYSTEM,SYSIDNT=LU62,                              *
       TRMTYPE=LUTYPE62,                                      *
       ACCMETH=VTAM,NETNAME=DGAAL01,                          *
       FEATURE=SINGLE,MODENAM=LU62,                           *
       OPERSEC=1,TRMSTAT=TRANSCEIVE,                          *
       TCTUAL=255,RUSIZE=256,BUFFER=256                       *
```

SYSIDNT defines the name by which this remote LU is to be known to CICS: it is this name that is passed to CICS TPs when started by a program on the PC. NETNAME refers to an LU name defined in VTAM, and MODENAM should be the same as the DLOGMOD defined in VTAM for this LU.

The process programming table and program control table between them define the TPs that can be run locally. These are the DFHPPT and DFHPCT. Typical CICS PPT and PCT entries are:

```
*
* CICS DFHPPT DEFINITION
*
  DFHPPT TYPE=ENTRY,PROGRAM=RECVLU62,                         X
         PGMLANG=COBOL,PGMSTAT=ENABLED,RES=NO
*
* CICS DFHPCT DEFINITION
*
  DFHPCT TYPE=ENTRY,PROGRAM=RECVLU62,                         X
         TRANSID=RECV,TWASIZE=160,                            X
         CLASS=LONG,TCLASS=NO,TRANSEC=1,                      X
         TRNPRTY=1,DTB=NO,RESTART=NO,                         X
```

```
DUMP=YES,RTIMOUT=0100,DTIMOUT=NO,                    X
SPURGE=YES,TPURGE=YES,                               X
TRNSTAT=ENABLED
```

The name given by TRANSID is the name by which the TP
is known, and is that used by remote TPs when establishing a conversation.

5.4 AVS CPI-C CONFIGURATION

To understand what is involved in the installation and
configuration of AVS in a VM system it is necessary to
understand something of VM and how various components interact. It is not the intention here to give a
tutorial on how to set up and configure VM, just to give
enough of the concepts so that communications programmers with a PC background can follow what their mainframe colleagues are talking about.

A VM system (e.g. a 4381 running VM/SP) runs a
program called control program (CP). This controls the
invocation of and communications between the various
virtual machines. Each of these runs its own copy of an
operating system, either conversational monitor system
(CMS) or group control system (GCS). Most virtual
machines run CMS; only certain special components need
the facilities of GCS.

The SAA method for programs to communicate between
CMS systems (i.e. between individual virtual machines
within one real one) is using APPC/VM via transparent
services access facility (TSAF). To communicate with
programs running on other non-VM computers in an SNA
network, there has to be a gateway system available to
take the APPC/VM connection managed by TSAF and
connect with other systems using LU 6.2.

APPC/VM VTAM support (AVS) is that gateway
server. It runs in a GCS machine and allows CMS systems
which use the CPI-C interface to APPC-VM to access
programs through VTAM using LU 6.2. In a basic
configuration AVS is set up as a global gateway giving
access into and out of a set of global resources, these
resources being CPI-C programs running in other CMS
systems. It is also possible to set up private gateways to
provide access to private resources.

These gateways are LUs to SNA, just like CICS. Thus in the VTAM definitions they are defined using an APPL definition.

Connections out of CPI-C are made by referring to symbolic destinations. These are mapped to the destination LU name, mode name, TP name and security requirements using the CMS communications directory file. This contains a list of entries as follows:

```
:NICK.nickname   :LUNAME.LU-name-qualifier target-LU
                 :TPN.transaction-program-name
                 :MODENAME.mode-name
                 :SECURITY.security-type
                 :USERID.user-id
                 :PASSWORD.password
```

Nickname is the name used by the CPI-C program to identify the resource. The LU-name-qualifier is the name of the AVS gateway used to access the SNA network. Target-LU is the name of the LU to be contacted. This LU name is, in SNA terms, an unqualified LU name: that is, it is not qualified by a network name. If the LU is not in the same domain as the AVS system then the name has to be translated by VTAM. Mode-name is the MODEENT to use, and security-type is NONE, SAME, or PGM. Only NONE and PGM are valid for LU 6.2 conversations through an AVS gateway.

5.5 GLOBAL AND PRIVATE RESOURCES AND GATEWAYS

A resource, identified in APPC by a TP name, can be defined in VM/SP as **local**, **global**, or **private**. Local resources are not available outside the system, and so are of no interest to us in discussing connection to PCs, etc.

Global resources can be accessed by incoming allocates that are routed through a global gateway. Global resources have to be active and waiting for inbound allocates for the connections to complete.

Private resources can also be accessed by incoming allocates, but these have to be routed through private gateways. There are two types of private gateway: dedicated and non-dedicated. A dedicated private gateway has a user id associated with it. The private resources accessed through a dedicated gateway always run in the virtual machine belonging to that user id. The private resources accessed through a non-dedicated private gateway run in the virtual machine belonging to the user id specified in the incoming allocate.

An incoming allocate to a private resource causes the appropriate virtual machine to be autologged if the machine is not already active.

5.5.1 Global resources

To create a global resource you must first authorize a virtual machine as a resource manager by adding to the machine's CP directory entry the following:

```
IUCV *INDENT resourceid GLOBAL
```

This allows that machine to define a resource whose name is `resourceid`. If `resourceid` is RESANY then the virtual machine can define any resource. For the resource to be defined, the machine must be active, and a program must have issued a `XCIDRM` command. This is described in Chapter 4.

5.5.2 Private resources

To create a private resource you must add the following to the server machine's CP directory entry:

```
IUCV ALLOW
IPL CMS
OPTION  MAXCONN nn
```

This allows the machine to define private resources. Nn is the maximum number of connections allowed for the virtual machine. Unless the programs are expected to handle several incoming conversations at once, or are going to make outbound connections once they have been started, then this number will be 1.

A virtual machine responsible for private resources may be autologged as a result of an incoming allocate. Therefore you need the following statements in your PROFILE EXEC:

```
SET SERVER ON
SET FULLSCREEN OFF
SET AUTOREAD OFF
```

Finally, you need to define a list of resources and the program associated with each. You also need to specify a list of user ids that are authorized to access each resource. This is done in the file $SERVER$ NAMES. This file consists of a set of entries as follows:

```
:NICK.resourceid
:LIST.user-id [user-id user-id . . .]
:MODULE.program
```

Resourceid is the name of the resource. This is the transaction name that is specified in incoming allocates that are routed to this resource. The user ids specified are the only users allowed to access this resource. If you want general access to this resource, specify * in place of the user-id list. Program is the name of the program to be started as a result of an incoming allocate for this resource.

5.5.3 Global gateways

A global gateway is activated by the command

```
AGW ACTIVATE GATEWAY gateway-name GLOBAL
```

Gateway-name is the name of the global gateway, and is the name used in the VTAM APPL statement. This is the LU name used to access the global resources defined in this system. There is no point in defining more than one global gateway.

5.5.4 Private gateways

There are two types of private gateway: dedicated and non-dedicated as described above. To activate a private dedicated gateway issue the command:

```
AGW ACTIVATE GATEWAY gateway PRIVATE USERID user-id
```

User-id is the user ID of the virtual machine which runs

the TPs started as a result of allocates coming in through this gateway.

To activate a private non-dedicated gateway, issue a similar command, but without specifying the USERID.

5.6   IMS CONFIGURATION

Until IMS v3.2, IMS itself could not handle LU 6.2 connections. There is, however, an option for IMS to provide a bridge between LU 6.2 and LU 6.1 which IMS can handle. This does not provide a complete APPC, but does provide a quite sufficient subset. The configuration has therefore to take account of the APPC bridge to IMS connection, the connection of the LU 6.2 LUs to VTAM, and the mapping of the LUs to IMS terminal definitions, (SUBPOOLs).

The LU 6.2 LUs that connect to IMS and the APPC bridge itself are defined to IMS using a stage 1 definition similar to the example shown below:

```
TYPE  UNITYPE=LUTYPE6,FPBUF=300,OUTBUF=300
      TERMINAL NAME=APPCBRDG
      OPTIONS=TRANRESP,NOMTOMSG),
      COMPT1=(SINGL1,VLVB),SESSION=20
*
      VTAMPOOL
*
      SUBPOOL NAME=DGAAL01
      NAME    DGAAL01
      SUBPOOL NAME=DGAAL02
      NAME    DGAAL02
*
```

Note that DGAAL01 and DGAAL02 are the names of the LUs in the PC. These LUs should be defined in VTAM just as described above for the VTAM definitions needed for CICS.

The VTAM definitions needed, besides the LINE, PU and LU definitions, which are very much like the one for CICS, are the APPL definition for the bridge:

```
APPCBRDG APPL ACBNAME=APPCBRDG                              X
              AUTH=(ACQ),                                   X
              EAS=20,                                       X
```

```
MODETAB=DGAMODE                                            X
PARSESS=YES
```

and the definitions of the modes to be used for the LU 6.1 connection between IMS and the bridge, and the LU 6.2 connection between the remote LUs and the bridge. The MODEENT for connection to the PC can be the same as for a connection to CICS.

```
* Mode table entry for IMS to bridge sessions
LU62NEGPS MODEENT LOGMODE=LU62NEGPS                        X
          TYPE=0,        NEGOTIATED BIND                   X
          FMPROF=X'12' FM PROFILE 18                       X
          TSPROF=X'04' TS PROFILE 4                        X
          PRIPROT=X'B1'                                    X
          SECPROT=X'B1'                                    X
          COMPROT=X'70A0'                                  X
          RUSIZES=X'F8F8'                                  X
          PSERVIC=X'060038000000380000000000'
```

5.7 AS/400 CONFIGURATION

In general, the AS/400 is configured as an **Advanced peer-to-peer networking** (APPN) network node. In this case, the AS/400 does not need to be told about the definition of LUs of the PC attaching to it: the description will be autoconfigured. However, you do need to define the PU definition of the PC to the AS/400.

The controller description parameters that are used when attaching a PC directly to an AS/400 are the following:

APPN   APPN capable. Set to *YES.

RMTNETID   Remote network identifier. Set to *NETATR. The network part of the partner LU names in the PC's definitions and the network name in the PC's PU definition must be set to the name given to the AS/400 in the LCLNETID parameter on the CHGNETA command. The default value for this on the AS/400 is "APPN".

RMTCPNAME   Remote control point name. Set to the name given to the PC's PU.

EXCHID   Exchange identifier. For dial lines this must match the PC's XID. The first three digits of the XID for OS/2 are 05D.

STNADR   Station address. Any value from 01 to FE. This must match the station address given in the PC's definition. This is only for SDLC lines.

NODETYPE   APPN node type. Set to *ENDNODE.

If the PC is being connected through a VTAM network then no changes need to be made to the AS/400 configuration to describe the PC.

Generally, you will be using the default LU (local location) on the AS/400. This has the same name as the PU or local control point name, which is given by the LCLCPNAME parameter on the CHGNETA command. By default this is Snnnnnnn where nnnnnnn is the serial number of the AS/400.

The mode entry on the PC has to match a mode description on the AS/400. A mode entry on the AS/400 is created using the command CRTMODD. The parameters on that command are as follows:

MODD   The mode description name. This is the name used to refer to this mode.

COS   Class of service. This refers to the priority assigned to sessions started with this mode. There is no equivalent on the PC.

MAXSSN   Maximum number of sessions. This should be the same as that parameter on the mode definition on the PC.

MAXCNV   Maximum number of conversations. This should be the same as the maximum-number-of-TPs parameter on the PC.

LCLCTLSSN   Minimum number for session controlled locally, i.e. contention winners. This should be the same as the contention-winners (target) parameter on the PC.

INPACING and OUTPACING   These should be the same as the OUTPACING and INPACING parameters on the PC.

MAXLENRU   This should be the same as the MAXRULEN parameter on the PC.

To establish an outbound connection from an AS/400 program you need to define an APPN location list. This is done using the CRTCFGL command. To create a remote connection provide an entry of the form

```
APPN remote-location-name (APPNRMTE)
```

Remote-location-name is the name by which the remote location is known to programs running on this node. The remote connection is defined by the values provided on the APPNRMTE parameter as follows:

Remote location name	The name of the remote location, i.e. the partner LU name.
Network identifier	The name of the network the remote LU is in, i.e. the network qualifier of the partner LU.
Local location name	The name of the local location or local LU. The default is the LU whose name is the same as the local PU, i.e. Snnnnnnn.
Location password	Specifies the password to be used for this LU-LU pair. This is only used if LU-LU session security is wanted.
Secure location	*YES if conversation-level security is used, *NO otherwise.

Control-point-name and control-point-network-identifier need not be specified as the partner LU name is given.

5.8 COMMUNICATIONS MANAGER CONFIGURATION

Most of the time the communications manager is quite invisible to users of systems which communicate using APPC. The only time that anyone needs to use the communications manager directly is when a new configuration is needed. This should be a rare occurrence as it is possible to tailor a template configuration file without having to go through all the agony of a full-blown configuration exercise. However, there are some occasions when a completely new configuration is needed, and anyway someone has to produce the template configurations for others to tailor.

The communications manager keeps its configurations in files in its home directory. These files all have the extension .CFG. To produce a new configuration, a copy has to be made of an existing configuration file. An empty configuration file is supplied with the communications manager for this purpose: ACSCFGUS.CFG. If this file is copied to another file in C:/CMLIB, say CICSCFG.CFG, then this configuration file can be modified from the communications manager by selecting Configure from the Advanced menu, and specifying CICSCFG as the configuration name.

For APPC connections, the following profiles will need to be configured:

- Workstation profile.
- SNA feature profile.
- LAN feature profile.
- X.25 feature profile.

The LAN features and X.25 features only need configuring if the PC is to be attached using token-ring or X.25.

Within SNA feature profiles there are several subprofiles that need configuring:

- SNA base profile.
- SDLC DLC adapter profile.
- Transmission service mode profile.
- Initial session limit profile.
- Local LU profile.
- Partner LU profile.
- Transaction program profile.

The SDLC DLC adapter obviously only needs configuring if the PC is to be attached using SDLC. The TP profile only needs configuring if the PC is to accept incoming allocates, i.e. if it is to act as a server of some sort.

5.8.1. Workstation profile

Figure 5.1 Changing workstation profile panel

```
┌──────────────────────────────────────────────────────────┐
│                  Change Workstation Profile               │
│                                                            │
│  Comment  . . . . . . . . . . . . . . . . . . . . . . . .  │
│     [APPC Configuration file for XYZ                    ]  │
│  Machine type  . . . . . . . . . . . . . . .   [0000]      │
│  Machine serial number  . . . . . . . . . . .  [0000000]   │
│  Machine model number . . . . . . . . . . . .  [000]       │
│  IBM plant of manufacture  . . . . . . . . . . [00]        │
│                                                            │
│  Translation table file name  . . . . . . . .  [ACSGTAB.DAT ] │
│  Error log file name  . . . . . . . . . . . . .            │
│     [ERROR.DAT                                       ⌒  ]  │
│  Error log size  . . . . . . . . . . . . . . . [16] K      │
│  Error log overflow option  . . . . . . . . ▸ Wrap         │
│                                             ▪ Extend       │
│                                                            │
│  Message log file name  . . . . . . . . . . . .            │
│     [MESSAGE.DAT                                        ]  │
│  Message log size . . . . . . . . . . . . . .  [500] messages │
│  Message log overflow option  . . . . . . . ▸ Wrap         │
│                                             ▪ Extend       │
│  Auto-start . . . . . . . . . . . . . . . . . ▸ Yes    ▪ No │
└──────────────────────────────────────────────────────────┘
```

There are two options that may need to be changed in the workstation profile (see Fig. 5.1). These are the translation table file name, and the autostart option. The translation table file name must be set or the convert verb described in Chapter 3 does not work. ACSGTAB is a supplied translation table. Others may be constructed as national language characteristics dictate.

The autostart option should be set to Yes, which will cause some more screens to be presented asking what should be started. There are several features that can be started. These can be started or not as needed, but clearly APPC must be. The machine type, serial number, etc. are only used in error messages that may be sent from the PC to NetView. However, it is good practice to complete these fields since, in some cases, problem determination is made easier.

5.8.2 SNA feature profile

The panels brought up by selecting this option on the main configuration panel are the ones pertaining to LU 6.2. You need to define the SNA base profile, the DLC profiles, and one or more LUs and partner LUs. When defining the LUs and partner LUs, you are constrained to define things in a certain order. First define your local LUs. Then define your transmission service modes and session limits, and then you can define your partner LUs. The TPs can be defined at any time. The reason for this is quite simple. The definition of partner LUs use the transmission service mode definitions and session limit definitions as resources to be referenced. If they have not yet been defined, they cannot be referenced and the partner LUs cannot be defined. Similarly partner LUs 'belong' to a particular LU. As this is a many-to-one relationship (one LU can reference many partner LUs, but any partner LU belongs to only one LU), the simplest place to make the reference is in the definition of the partner LU. Therefore the local LU should be defined first.

SNA base profile.

Figure 5.2 Change SNA base panel

```
               Change SNA Base Profile

Physical unit (PU) name . . . . . . . . . . . . . . . . .    [DGAPUL   ]
Network name . . . . . . . . . . . . . . . . . . . . . . . .    [         ]
Node ID (in hex) . . . . . . . . . . . . . . . . . . . . .    [00000]
Auto-activate APPC attach manager . . . . . . . .  ▶  Yes
                                                    ■  No
```

Traditionally, the PU name was used very little in LU 6.2, really only in error messages. However, it is becoming more important with APPN, and therefore must be set (see Fig. 5.2). It is particularly important when communicating with APPC nodes such as the AS/400. It should be set to the same name as the PU name defined to VTAM. The network name is the name of the local domain, and should only be left blank in a single domain network. The node id field is the XID, and must be set for dial-up links. It must be noted that the block number for OS/2 communication manager is 05D and cannot be changed. The APPC attach manager should be set to autoactivate where the OS/2 machine receives allocates, that is, where it is a service provider.

SDLC DLC adapter profile

Figure 5.3 Change SDLC DLC adapter profile panel

```
┌─────────────────────────────────────────────────────────┐
│          Create/Change SDLC DLC Adapter Profile          │
│                                                           │
│ Adapter Number  ....................:    0                │
│ Load DLC  .........................  ▶ Yes   ■ No        │
│ Free unused link  ..................  ■ Yes   ▶ No       │
│                                                           │
│ Maximum RU size  ...................    [256 ] bytes     │
│ Send window count  .................    [7]              │
│ Receive window count  ..............    [7]              │
│                                                           │
│ Line type  .........................  ■ Switched  ......  │
│                                       ▶ Non-switched     │
│ Link station role  .................  ▶ Secondary  ..... │
│                                       ■ Primary  ....... │
│                                       ■ Negotiable  ..... │
│                                                           │
│ Line mode  .........................                      │
│    ▶  Line turnaround required                            │
│    ■  Constant request to send                            │
│                                                           │
│ NRZI  ..............................  ▶ Yes   ■ No       │
│ Modem rate  ........................  ▶ Full speed       │
│                                       ■ Half speed       │
└─────────────────────────────────────────────────────────┘
```

There are several points to make about the fields on this panel (see Fig. 5.3):

1 You may not want to specify a free unused link on a switched line into an SNA network: the link will be taken down 30 seconds after it becomes established if no conversation is set up in that time.

2 You must specify station role secondary if you are attaching to a mainframe host.

3 The RU size must be exactly 9 less than MAXDATA as specified in the VTAM PU definition.

4 Send window count and receive window count must be the same as MAXOUT and PASSLIM as given in the VTAM PU definition or MAXOUT from the AS/400 definition. For modem lines, NRZI and modem rate must also agree with the NCP configuration.

Transmission service mode profile

Figure 5.4 Change transmission service level profile panel (1)

```
      Create/Change Transmission Service Level Profile

Mode name  ..............................:    DGAMODE


Comment  ................................
    [Mode for use with CICS                       ]
Minimum RU size .........................     [256  ]
Maximum RU size  ........................     [256  ]
Receive pacing limit ....................     [5 ]
Session Limit  ..........................     [1    ]
```

The mode name and characteristics (see Fig. 5.4) must match the relevant VTAM parameters or mode characteristics from the AS/400. The minimum and maximum RU sizes have to be the same, and must match the RUSIZES parameter. The RUSIZES parameter is encoded as described above. The receive pacing limit must match the PSNDPAC parameter from the VTAM definition, or the OUTPACING value from the AS/400 mode definition. If this parameter does not match then the session fails erratically, especially when large blocks of data are sent. For conventional connection to CICS, the session limit should be set to 1. For parallel sessions support, VTAM and NCP must have support for independent LUs. For attaching to CMS machines via AVS, or to an AS/400, set the session limit to a number other than 1, say 8.

If the session limit is not 1 then you also need a mode called SNASVCMG. This mode is used by SNA to negotiate session parameters, and is automatically defined for you if you have defined any parallel session modes, but if you want, you can define it explicitly. It should be defined as shown in Fig. 5.5. It is not needed when you have single-session LUs for connection to CICS. The session limit for SNASVCMG must be 1 or 2.

Figure 5.5 Change transmission service level profile panel (2)

```
Create/Change Transmission Service Level Profile

Mode name ............................. : SNASVCMG

Comment ...................................
  [Mode for negotiating with VTAM or AS/400          ]
Minimum RU size .......................... [256  ]
Maximum RU size .......................... [256  ]
Receive pacing limit ...................... [5 ]
Session Limit ............................. [2    ]
```

If you are using parallel sessions, the SNASVCMG mode is automatically defined for you with a session limit of 2, and if you do not define SNASVCMG explicitly then 2 is added to the session limit of the partner LUs using parallel sessions (unless this takes them over their limit of 255).

Initial session limit profile

Figure 5.6 Change initial session limit profile panel (1)

```
┌─────────────────────────────────────────────────────────────┐
│          Create/Change Initial Session Limit Profile         │
│                                                              │
│ Initial session limit profile ...................:   NORMAL  │
│                                                              │
│ Comment  .................................                   │
│   [Initial Session Limits                         ]          │
│                                                              │
│ Minimum number of                                            │
│   contention winners source .................     [0 ]       │
│                                                              │
│ Minimum number of                                            │
│   contention winners target ..................    [0 ]       │
│                                                              │
│ Number of automatically                                      │
│   activated sessions .........................    [0  ]      │
└─────────────────────────────────────────────────────────────┘
```

This profile controls how many sessions the communications manager attempts to start when it is started itself, and, for parallel sessions, how many are under direct local control and how many are to be controlled by the partner LU. The number of contention winner source sessions is the number of sessions that can be allocated by the local LU to the partner LU. Similarly, the number of contention winners target is the number of sessions that the partner LU can allocate. If the local LU needs to allocate a session when it has used all its contention winner sessions, it has to ask the partner LU to allocate a session for it. This can take longer than allocating a contention winner session. Indeed, the number of contention winners is purely an optimization parameter. The session limit profile shown in Fig 5.6 is absolutely safe: it will work with any LU, mode and partner LU, with the exception of MODE SNASVCMG, which you do not use with CICS. The parameters for SNASVCMG are shown in Fig. 5.7.

Figure 5.7 Change initial session limit profile panel (2)

```
┌─────────────────────────────────────────────────────────────┐
│          Create/Change Initial Session Limit Profile         │
│                                                              │
│ Initial session limit profile ....................: SNASVCMG │
│                                                              │
│ Comment ...................................                  │
│    [Initial Session Limits for SNASVCMG mode        ]        │
│                                                              │
│ Minimum number of                                            │
│    contention winners source ................. [1  ]         │
│                                                              │
│ Minimum number of                                            │
│    contention winners target .................. [1  ]        │
│                                                              │
│ Number of automatically                                      │
│    activated sessions ........................ [0  ]         │
└─────────────────────────────────────────────────────────────┘
```

Local LU profile

Figure 5.8 Change local LU profile panel

```
┌─────────────────────────────────────────────────────────────┐
│          Create/Change Local APPC Logical Unit Profile       │
│                                                              │
│  LU alias .............................. LU62001             │
│                                                              │
│  Comment ..............................                      │
│     [Local LU for talking to CICS                   ]        │
│                                                              │
│  LU name ............................. [DGAAL01 ]            │
│                                                              │
│  Default LU ............................ ■ Yes   ▶ No        │
│                                                              │
│  LU local address (NAU address) ........... [07]             │
│                                                              │
│  LU session limit ......................... [1  ]            │
│                                                              │
│  Maximum number of                                           │
│     transaction programs ................... [1  ]           │
└─────────────────────────────────────────────────────────────┘
```

The LU alias (see Fig. 5.8) is the name by which the LU is known locally. This is usually different from the VTAM or network name for the LU which is given by LU name. The reason for making them different is so that the same program can be used without alteration on several PCs which may have different LU names. The LU local address (NAU address) has to match the VTAM parameter LOCADDR in the LU definition. The LU session limit has to be at least as big as the total needed for all partner LUs defined, e.g. 1 for a CICS, or 10 (2 for SNASVCMG + 8 for the user mode) for one LU–LU session group connection to AVS or the AS/400. The maximum number of transaction programs for the LU should be the same as the total session limit excluding the SNASVCMG mode.

Partner LU profile

Figure 5.9 Change partner LU profile panels

```
                  Create/Change Partner LU Profile

    Partner LU alias . . . . . . . . . . . . . . . .:     CICS1
    Comment   . . . . . . . . . . . . . . . . . . .
      [CICS                                          ]
    Fully qualified
      partner LU name . . . . . . . . . . . .      [           ].[DGACICS1]
    Partner LU
      uninterpreted name . . . . . . . . . . .     [DGACICS1]
    LU alias . . . . . . . . . . . . . . . . . . . . .     [LU62001  ]
    DLC type . . . . . . . . . . . . . . . . . . . .
       ▶ SDLC. . .
       ■ IBM PC Networks
       ■ IBM Token-Ring Network
    Partner LU session limit . . . . . . . . .      [1    ]
    Maximum mapped conversation
      logical record length . . . . . . . . .      [32767] bytes
    LU-LU session security   . . . . . . . . .  ■ Yes          ▶ No
    Conversation security  . . . . . . . . . . .  ▶ Yes        ■ No
    Permanent connection   . . . . . . . . . .  ▶ Yes          ■ No
```

```
┌─────────────────────────────────────────┐
│         Add/Change a Mode Name           │
│                                          │
│  Mode name  . . . . . . . . . . [DGAMODE ] │
│                                          │
│  Initial session limit                   │
│     profile name . . . . . . . . [NORMAL   ] │
└─────────────────────────────────────────┘
```

The partner LU fully qualified name (see Fig. 5.9) is the name on the APPL statement in the VTAM definitions that defines CICS, preceded by the domain name. The uninterpreted name is either the same as the second part of the fully qualified name or is a local name defined in an interpret table. The LU alias field specifies the local LU used to connect to this partner LU. The partner LU session limit must be greater than or equal to the number of sessions needed for all the modes defined, e.g. 1 for a single-session connection to CICS, or more typically, 10 for an AVS or AS/400 connection (2 for the SNASVCMG mode and 8 for the user mode). The mapped conversation logical record length field should be set to the length of the maximum record size to be sent, or if you are uncertain, to 32767. LU–LU session security must match the VTAM definition.

You must define all modes you are to use with a partner LU. Typically, you will only be using one if you are connecting to CICS, or one user mode plus SNASVCMG if you are connecting to AVS or an AS/400. The SNASVCMG mode is automatically added for you if you are using parallel sessions.

Transaction program profile

Locally started TPs do not need to be registered with the communications manager, so if all the programs to be run on the PC are to be started manually then you do not need to worry about the TP configuration. If a program is going to be started by a remote TP, it must be configured into the communications manager (see Fig. 5.10), just as CICS TPs have to be entered in the PCT.

Clearly, the communications manager has to know the name of the TP as it is known to the remote program, and the name of the file containing the executable. It also needs to know how to start the program – whether the program is a presentation manager program, etc. It also needs to know whether it should start the program each time a start request is received or whether one invocation of the executable will do. This is addressed in more detail in the section on programming APPC on the PC in Chapter 4.

Figure 5.10 Change transaction program profile panels

```
┌──────────────────────────────────────────────────────────────┐
│  Create/Change Remotely Attachable Transaction Program Profile │
│                                                                │
│  TP profile name  . . . . . . . . . . . . . . . . . . . . . :   SEND          │
│  Comment . . . . . . . . . . . . . . . . . . . . . . . . .    │
│     [Local TP                            ]                     │
│  TP filespec . . . . . . . . . . . . . . . . . . . . . . .    │
│     [C:\CICSTEST\SEND.EXE                              ]       │
│  Service TP  . . . . . . . . . . . . . . . . . . . . . . .  ■ Yes    ▶ No      │
│                                                                │
│  ┌──────────────────────────────────────────────────────┐    │
│  │  TP name                                              │    │
│  │  [SEND                                            ]    │    │
│  └──────────────────────────────────────────────────────┘    │
└──────────────────────────────────────────────────────────────┘

┌──────────────────────────────────────────────────────────────┐
│  Sync level  . . . . . . . . . . . . . . . . . . . . . . .  ▶  Confirm        │
│                                                            ■  None           │
│                                                            ■  Either         │
│  Conversation type  . . . . . . . . . . . . . . . . . . .  ■  Basic          │
│                                                            ▶  Mapped         │
│                                                            ■  Either         │
│  Conversation security  . . . . . . . . . . . . . . . . .  ■ Yes    ▶ No      │
│  TP operation  . . . . . . . . . . . . . . . . . . . . . .                    │
│     ■ Queued – attach manager started. . .                     │
│     ■ Queued – operator started. . .                           │
│     ▶ Non-queued – attach manager started. . .                 │
│  ┌──────────────────────────────────────────────────────┐    │
│  │  TP start-up Parameters . . . . . . . . . . . . . . . . .   │
│  │  [                            ]                        │    │
│  │  Program Type . . . . . . . . . . . . . . . . . . . . . .   │
│  │     ▶    Presentation Manager (Windowed)              │    │
│  │     ■   VIO-Windowable                                │    │
│  │     ■   Full Screen (Separate screen group)           │    │
│  │     ■   Background                                    │    │
│  └──────────────────────────────────────────────────────┘    │
└──────────────────────────────────────────────────────────────┘
```

**5.9 BATCH
CONFIGURATION**

Configuration is too complicated to be carried out from scratch for each PC. Generally there is a set of standard template configurations which can easily be added to the VTAM definition. There should also be a set of standard configuration files that can be installed on PCs. Such standard configurations will, in general, need only minor changes: new PU names and XIDs, for instance. There is a mechanism within the communication manager to assist the production of tailored configurations: the **batch configurator**.

The batch configurator takes as input a configuration file and a modification script that describes what new configuration files are to be produced and how they are to differ from the input configuration file. Very few parameters can be changed: the batch configurator is not intended to replace the interactive configuration of the communication manager. However, the sort of things that are likely to vary from one PC to another within the same environment can be changed, e.g. PU name, token-ring address or XID.

The batch configurator can also be used to add partner LUs and local LUs by copying then modifying existing profiles. This means that if a new service is added then the communication manager configurations can easily be updated as part of installing the new programs.

A typical modification script is shown below. It defines the name of the new configuration file being generated (the FNM record), a new comment field (the COM record), sets the PU name and XID (the SNA record), and a new token-ring address (the TRN record).

```
FNM PS212345
COM this is the configuration for PS/2 12345
SNA PS212345,          ,12345
TRN 00,400000012345
```

In any large installation the control of configuration is under the control of network staff, and typically only a few standard configurations are used, just as with 3270 terminals. The apparent difficulty of configuring APPC connections is only real the first time. From then on, configuration is a largely routine exercise not requiring much thought. The users of systems which use both PCs and mainframes that communicate using APPC will often be unaware that any communications are taking place, just as users are often unaware when they are using files on a network file server. This degree of blissful ignorance is a good thing, and one that is difficult to achieve using other less-structured PC/host communications methods such as 3270 connections.

Indeed the programming of APPC applications also becomes almost intuitive after a little practice. The architecture is fundamentally simple.

REFERENCES FOR VTAM CONFIGURATION

Advance Communications Function for VTAM version 3 Installation and Resource Definition (VMS, VSE and VM), IBM Corporation, Research Triangle Park, NC, September 1985.

Network Program Products Samples: Netview, IBM Corporation, Research Triangle Park, NC, December 1989.

REFERENCE FOR CICS CONFIGURATION

Customer Information Control System/DOS/VS Version 1.7 Intercommunication Facilities Guide, IBM Corporation, Mechanicsburgh, PA, July 1987.

REFERENCE FOR AVS CONFIGURATION

Virtual Machine/System Product Release 6, Connectivity Planning, Administration and Operation, IBM Corporation, Mechanicsburgh, PA, October 1988.

REFERENCE FOR AS/400 CONFIGURATION

AS/400 Communications: Advanced Program–to–Program Communications and Advanced Peer–to–Peer Networking User's Guide, IBM Corporation, Rochester, NY, September 1989.

REFERENCE FOR IMS CONFIGURATION

IMS LU 6.1 Adapter for LU 6.2 Applications: Program description/Operations Manual, IBM Corporation, San Jose, CA, December 1989.

REFERENCES FOR COMMUNICATION MANAGER CONFIGURATION

IBM Operating System/2 Extended Edition Version 1.3 Administrator's Guide for Communications, IBM Corporation, Boca Raton FL, January 1991.

Appendix A
Sample Programs

The basic program consists of a single program written in C which runs on the PC, and two CICS transactions which are invoked by the PC program.

The protocol used between the PC program and the two transactions is typical of the sort you are likely to meet: in one case the PC submits data to the CICS TP LU62SUB which either rejects the data and sends an error message or issues a confirmation. In the other case the PC program sends a request to the CICS TP LU62RET which either rejects the request and sends an error message, or sends a reply to the PC which then either rejects the reply and sends an error message or issues a confirmation. The interaction with LU62SUB is illustrated at the end of Chapter 3, and the interaction with LU62RET is illustrated at the end of Chapter 2.

The PC program uses the include file appc.h and the following subroutines:

```
APPC_MC_allocate
APPC_MC_confirmed
APPC_MC_deallocate
APPC_MC_receive_and_wait
APPC_MC_send_data
APPC_tp_ended
APPC_tp_started
convert
```

all of which are listed in Appendix B.

A.1   PMSAMP.C   This is the foreground thread to the OS/2 requester
program.

```c
#define INCL_DOSPROCESS
#define INCL_WINDIALOGS
#define INCL_WINMENUS
#define INCL_WINFRAMEMGR
#define INCL_WINSYS
#define INCL_WINENTRYFIELDS
#include <os2.h>           // the PM header file
#include <string.h>        // C/2 string functions
#include "pmsamp.h"        // Resource symbolic identifiers
#include "record.h"
#include <stdlib.h>


// Function prototype
MRESULT EXPENTRY WindowProc(HWND hwnd, USHORT msg, MPARAM mpl, MPARAM mp2);
MRESULT EXPENTRY SubWindowProc(HWND hwnd, USHORT msg, MPARAM mpl, MPARAM mp2);
MRESULT EXPENTRY SendDlgProc(HWND hwnd, USHORT msg, MPARAM mpl, MPARAM mp2);
MRESULT EXPENTRY RetrieveDlgProc(HWND hwnd, USHORT msg, MPARAM mpl, MPARAM mp2);
void boxtext(HPS hps, int x, int y, int dx, int dy, char *name, char *text);
void waitmsgon(void);
void waitmsgoff(void);
int pascal checkreply();


VOID cdecl main(VOID);
                        // Define parameters by type
HAB   hab;              // Anchor block handle
HMQ   hmq;              // Message queue handle
HWND      hwndClient;   // Client window handle
HWND      hwndSubFrame =(HWND)NULL;
HWND      hwndSubClient = (HWND)NULL;
ULONG     flCreate = FCF_STANDARD; // Frame control flag
BOOL      bComplete = FALSE;      // Switch for first time through
HWND      hwndFrame;             // Frame window handle
char      message[80];
char      szMBtitle[80];          // Message box title
char      NameStr[16];
char      AddressStr[16];
char      PostCodeStr[16];
char      CountryStr[16];


ULONG ThreadSem = 0;
HSEM  hsemThreadSem = &ThreadSem;
VOID FAR appcjob(VOID);
VOID enablefns(void);
VOID disablefns(void);
int  fnsavail = TRUE;


/********************** Start of main procedure **********************/
```

```
VOID cdecl main( )
{
    QMSG    qmsg;
    char        threadstack[4096];
    TID tidPrn;

    hab = WinInitialize(NULL);
    hmq = WinCreateMsgQueue(hab, 0);
    DosCreateThread(appcjob, &tidPrn, &threadstack[4094]);

    WinRegisterClass(          // Register Window Class
        hab,                   // Anchor block handle
        "MyWindow",            // Window Class name
        WindowProc,            // Address of Window Procedure
        CS_SIZEREDRAW.         // Class Style
        0                      // No extra window words
        ):

    hwndFrame = WinCreateStdWindow(
        HWND_DESKTOP, // Desktop Window is parent
        0,              // Frame Style
        &flCreate,      // Frame Control Flag
        "MyWindow",     // Window Class name
        "",             // No window title
        OL,             // Client style of visible
        NULL,           // Resource is in .EXE file
        ID_PMSAMP,      // Frame window identifier
        (PHWND)&hwndClient // Client window handle
        );
    WinSetWindowPos(hwndFrame,
        HWND_TOP,
        100, 35,
        410, 300,
        SWP_SIZE | SWP_MOVE | SWP_ACTIVATE | SWP_SHOW);
    WinQueryWindowText(hwndFrame, sizeof(szMBtitle), szMBtitle);
    WinLoadString(hab, NULL, IDS_NAME, sizeof(NameStr), (PSZ)NameStr);
    WinLoadString(hab, NULL, IDS_ADDRESS, sizeof(AddressStr), (PSZ)AddressStr);
    WinLoadString(hab, NULL, IDS_POSTCODE,
                         sizeof(PostCodeStr), (PSZ)PostCodeStr);
    WinLoadString(hab, NULL, IDS_COUNTRY, sizeof(CountryStr), (PSZ)CountryStr);
/*****************************************************************************/
/* Get and dispatch messages from the application message queue            */
/* until WinGetMsg returns FALSE, indicating a WM_QUIT message.            */
/*****************************************************************************/
    while(WinGetMsg(hab, (PQMSG)&qmsg, (HWND)NULL, 0,0 ))
        WinDispatchMsg(hab, (PQMSG)&qmsg);

    WinDestroyWindow(hwndFrame);     // Tidy up...
    WinDestroyMsgQueue(hmq);         // and
    WinTerminate(hab);               // terminate the application
    }
/********************* End of main procedure *********************/
```

```
/********************* Start of window procedure *********************/
MRESULT EXPENTRY WindowProc (HWND hwnd, USHORT msg, MPARAM mpl, MPARAM mp2)
{
    HPS hps;        // Presentation space handle
    POINTL pt;      // String screen coordinates
    RECTL rc;       // Window rectangle

    switch( msg )
    {
    case WM_CREATE:         // Window initialization
        break;
    case WM_COMMAND:
        switch (SHORT1FROMMP(mpl))
        {
        case ID_EXIT:
        case IDA_EXIT:
            WinLoadString(hab, NULL, IDS_EXIT, sizeof(message), (PSZ)message);
            if(WinMessageBox(HWND_DESKTOP,
                    hwndFrame,
                    (PSZ)message,
                    (PSZ)szMBtitle,
                    (USHORT)NULL,
                    MB_YESNO | MB_CUAWARNING |
                    MB_APPLMODAL) == MBID_YES)
            /**************************************/
            /* PS resources are tidied in WM_DESTROY */
            /**************************************/
            {
                record.cmd = ID_EXIT;
                DosSemClear(hsemThreadSem);
                WinPostMsg(hwnd, WM_CLOSE, OL, OL);
                }
            break;

        case ID_SEND:
            if (!fnsavail)
                break;
            WinDlgBox(HWND_DESKTOP,        // Place anywhere on desktop
                hwndFrame,                 // Owned by frame
                SendDlgProc,               // Address of dialog procedure
                NULL,                      // Module handle
                DLG_SEND,                  // Dialog identifier in resource
                NULL);                     // Initialization data
            waitmsgon();
            record.cmd = ID_SEND;
            DosSemClear(hsemThreadSem);
            bComplete = TRUE;
            break;

        case ID_RETRIEVE:
            if (!fnsavail)
                break;
```

```
            WinDlgBox(HWND_DESKTOP,          // Place anywhere on desktop
                 hwndFrame,                  // Owned by frame
                 RetrieveDlgProc,            // Address of dialog procedure
                 NULL,                       // Module handle
                 DLG_RETRIEVE,               // Dialog identifier in resource
                 NULL);                      // Initialization data
            bComplete = TRUE;
            record.cmd = ID_RETRIEVE;
            DosSemClear(hsemThreadSem);
            waitmsgon();
            break

        case ID_HELP:
            {
                CHAR        szHlp[300];

                WinLoadString(hab, NULL, IDS_HELP, sizeof(szHlp),
                                    (PSZ)szHlp);
                WinMessageBox(HWND_DESKTOP,
                        hwndFrame,
                        (PSZ)szHlp,
                        (PSZ)szMBtitle,
                        (USHORT)NULL,
                        MB_CANCEL | MB_CUANOTIFICATION | MB_APPLMODAL);
                break;
                }
        case ID_ABOUT:
            {
                char        szHlp[300];

                WinLoadString(hab, NULL, IDS_ABOUT, sizeof(szHlp),
                                    (PSZ)szHlp);
                WinMessageBox(HWND_DESKTOP,
                        hwndFrame,
                        (PSZ)szHlp,
                        (PSZ)szMBtitle,
                        (USHORT)NULL,
                        MB_CANCEL | MB_CUANOTIFICATION | MB_APPLMODAL);
                break;
                }
        default:
            return WinDefWindowProc(hwnd, msg, mpl, mp2);
            }
        break;

case NO_COMMS:
    waitmsgoff();
    enablefns();
    WinLoadString(hab, NULL, IDS_NO_COMMS, sizeof(message), (PSZ)message);
    WinMessageBox(HWND_DESKTOP,
        hwndFrame,
        (PSZ)message,
```

```
            (PSZ)szMBtitle,
            (USHORT)NULL,
            MB_CANCEL | MB_CUACRITICAL | MB_APPLMODAL);
        WinPostMsg(hwnd, WM_CLOSE, OL, OL);
        break;

case DONE:
        waitmsgoff();
        enablefns();
        switch(record.rc)
        {
        case OK:
            bComplete = TRUE;
            break;

        case DONE_BUT:
            bComplete = TRUE;
            WinLoadString(hab, NULL, IDS_DONE_BUT,
                              sizeof(message), (PSZ)message);
            WinMessageBox(HWND_DESKTOP,
                hwndFrame,
                (PSZ)message,
                (PSZ)szMBtitle,
                (USHORT)NULL,
                MB_CANCEL | MB_CUAWARNING | MB_APPLMODAL);
            break;

        case RESOURCE_FAILURE:
            bComplete = FALSE;
            WinLoadString(hab, NULL, IDS_RESOURCEFAIL,
                              sizeof(message), (PSZ)message);
            WinMessageBox(HWND_DESKTOP,
                hwndFrame,
                (PSZ)message,
                (PSZ)szMBtitle,
                (USHORT)NULL,
                MB_CANCEL | MB_CUACRITICAL | MB_APPLMODAL);
            break;

        case CICS_ABENDED:
            bComplete = FALSE;
            WinLoadString(hab, NULL, IDS_CICSABEND
                              sizeof(message), (PSZ)message);
            WinMessageBox(HWND_DESKTOP,
                hwndFrame,
                (PSZ)message,
                (PSZ)szMBtitle,
                (USHORT)NULL,
                MB_CANCEL | MB_CUACRITICAL | MB_APPLMODAL);
            break;
```

```
     case CICS_ERROR_MESSAGE:
         bComplete = FALSE;
         WinMessageBox(HWND_DESKTOP,
              hwndFrame,
              (PSZ)record.message,
              (PSZ)szMBtitle,
              (USHORT)NULL,
              MB_CANCEL | MB_CUACRITICAL | MB_APPLMODAL);
         break;
         }
     WinInvalidateRegion(hwnd, NULL, FALSE); // Force a repaint
     break;

     case WM_PAINT:
     /******************************************************************/
     /* Window contents are drawn here. First time through, bComplete  */
     /* is FALSE, so window is simply filled with SYSCLR_WINDOW.       */
     /* On subsequent passes, if bComplete has been set to TRUE in the */
     /* dialog procedure, GpiCharStringAt draws the text.             */
     /******************************************************************/
         hps = WinBeginPaint(hwnd, (HPS)NULL, (PRECTL)&rc);
         WinFillRect(hps, (PRECTL)&rc, SYSCLR_WINDOW);
         if(bComplete)
         {
              boxtext(hps, 35, 183, 300, 20, NameStr, record.name);
              boxtext(hps, 35, 125, 300, 48, AddressStr, record.address[2]);
              pt.x = 38L; pt.y = 161L;      // Coordinates of location
              GpiCharStringAt(hps, &pt,
                       (LONG)strlen(record.address[0]), record.address[0]);
              pt.x =38L; pt.y = 146L;       // Coordinates of location
              GpiCharStringAt(hps, &pt,
                       (LONG)strlen(record.address[1]), record.address[1]);
              boxtext(hps, 35, 95, 300, 20, PostCodeStr, record.postcode);
              boxtext(hps, 35, 65, 300, 20, CountryStr, record.country);
              }
         WinEndPaint(hps);          // Drawing is complete
         break;

     case WM_CLOSE:
         WinPostMsg(hwnd, WM_QUIT, OL, OL);     // Cause termination
         break;

     default:
         return WinDefWindowProc(hwnd, msg, mpl, mp2);
         }
     return FALSE;
     }
/********************** End of window procedure **********************/

/********************** Start of dialog procedure **********************/
MRESULT EXPENTRY SendDlgProc(HWND hwndDlg, USHORT msg, MPARAM mpl, MPARAM mp2)
{
```

```
char       str[9];
char fname[65];
int  action;

switch (msg)
{
case WM_INITDLG:
    WinSendDlgItemMsg(hwndDlg,
        DLG_NAME,
        EM_SETTEXTLIMIT,
        MPFROMSHORT(sizeof(record.name)-1),
        MPFROMSHORT(NULL));
    WinSendDlgItemMsg(hwndDlg,
        DLG_ADDRESS1,
        EM_SETTEXTLIMIT,
        MPFROMSHORT(sizeof(record.address[0]-1),
        MPFROMSHORT(NULL));
    WinSendDlgItemMsg(hwndDlg,
        DLG_ADDRESS2,
        EM_SETTEXTLIMIT,
        MPFROMSHORT(sizeof(record.address[1])-1),
        MPFROMSHORT(NULL));
    WinSendDlgItemMsg(hwndDlg,
        DLG_ADDRESS3,
        EM_SETTEXTLIMIT,
        MPFROMSHORT(sizeof(record.address[2])-1),
        MPFROMSHORT(NULL));
    WinSendDlgItemMsg(hwndDlg,
        DLG_POSTCODE,
        EM_SETTEXTLIMIT,
        MPFROMSHORT(sizeof(record.postcode)-1),
        MPFROMSHORT(NULL));
    WinSendDlgItemMsg(hwndDlg,
        DLG_COUNTRY,
        EM_SETTEXTLIMIT,
        MPFROMSHORT(sizeof(record.country)-1),
        MPFROMSHORT(NULL));
    WinSetDlgItemText(hwndDlg, DLG_NAME, record.name);
    WinSetDlgItemText(hwndDlg, DLG_ADDRESS1, record.address[0]);
    WinSetDlgItemText(hwndDlg, DLG_ADDRESS2, record.address[1]);
    WinSetDlgItemText(hwndDlg, DLG_ADDRESS3, record.address[2]);
    WinSetDlgItemText(hwndDlg, DLG_POSTCODE, record.postcode);
    WinSetDlgItemText(hwndDlg, DLG_COUNTRY, record.country);
    break;

case WM_CONTROL:
    if( SHORT2FROMMP(mp1) == EN_KILLFOCUS)
    {
        short idDlgItem = SHORT1FROMMP(mp1);
        char      str[65];
        WinQueryDlgItemText(hwndDlg, idDlgItem, 65, str);
        strupr(str);
```

```
                WinSetDlgItemText(hwndDlg, idDlgItem, str);
            }
        break;

    case WM_COMMAND:      // Posted by pushbutton or key
    /*******************************************************************/
    /* PM sends a WM_COMMAND message when the user presses either  */
    /* the Enter or Escape pushbuttons.                           */
    /*******************************************************************/
        switch(SHORT1FROMMP(mp1))      // Extract the command value
        {
        case DID_OK:
            WinQueryDlgItemText(hwndDlg, DLG_NAME,
                                    sizeof(record.name), record.name);
            WinQueryDlgItemText(hwndDlg, DLG_ADDRESS1,
                        sizeof(record.address[0]), record.address[0]);
            WinQueryDlgItemText(hwndDlg, DLG_ADDRESS2,
                        sizeof(record.address[1]), record.address[1]);
            WinQueryDlgItemText(hwndDlg, DLG_ADDRESS3,
                        sizeof(record.address[2]), record.address[2]);
            WinQueryDlgItemText(hwndDlg, DLG_POSTCODE,
                        sizeof(record.postcode), record.postcode);
            WinQueryDlgItemText(hwndDlg, DLG_COUNTRY,
                        sizeof(record.country), record.country);
        case DID_CANCEL:      // The Cancel pushbutton or Escape key
            WinDismissDlg(hwndDlg, TRUE);      // Removes the dialog box
            return FALSE;

        default:
            break;
            }
        break;
    default:
        /*******************************************************************/
        /* Any event messages that the dialog procedure has not processed */
        /* come here and are processed by WinDefDlgProc.               */
        /* This call MUST exist in your dialog procedure.              */
        /*******************************************************************/
            return WinDefDlgProc(hwndDlg, msg, mp1, mp2);
            }
    return FALSE;
    }
/********************** End of dialog procedure **********************/

/********************** Start of dialog procedure **********************/
MRESULT EXPENTRY RetrieveDlgProc(HWND hwndDlg, USHORT msg,
                            MPARAM mp1, MPARAM mp2)
{
    char      str[9];
    char fname[65];
    int  action;
```

```
    switch (msg)
    {
    case WM_INITDLG:
        WinSendDlgItemMsg(hwndDlg,
            DLG_NAME,
            EM_SETTEXTLIMIT,
            MPFROMSHORT(sizeof(record.name)-1),
            MPFROMSHORT(NULL));
        WinSetDlgItemText(hwndDlg, DLG_NAME, record.name);
        break;

    case WM_CONTROL:
        if(SHORT2FROMMP(mpl) == EN_KILLFOCUS)
        {
            short idDlgItem = SHORT1FROMMP(mpl);
            char     str[65];

            WinQueryDlgItemText(hwndDlg, idDlgItem, 65, str);
            strupr(str);
            WinSetDlgItemText(hwndDlg, idDlgItem, str);
            }
        break;

    case WM_COMMAND:     // Posted by pushbutton or key
        switch(SHORT1FROMMP(mpl))          // Extract the command value
        {
        case DID_OK:
            WinQueryDlgItemText(hwndDlg, DLG_NAME,
                              sizeof(record.name), record.name);
        case DID_CANCEL:    // The Cancel pushbutton or Escape Key
            WinDismissDlg(hwndDlg, TRUE);   //Removes the dialog box
            return FALSE;
        default:
            break;
            }
        break;
    default
        return WinDefDlgProc(hwndDlg, msg, mpl, mp2);
        }
    return FALSE;
    }
/********************** End of dialog procedure **********************/

void boxtext(hps, x, y,  dx, dy, name, text)
HPS  hps;                 // Presentation space handle
int x;
int y;
int dx;
int dy;
char *name;
char *text;
{
```

```
      RECTL      rect;
      POINTL pt;              // String screen coordinates

      rect.xLeft = (long)x;
      rect.yBottom = (long)y;
      rect.xRight = (long)(x + dx);
      rect.yTop = (long)(y + dy);
      WinDrawBorder(hps, &rect, 1L, 1L, SYSCLR_WINDOWFRAME,
                                OL, DB_AREAATTRS | DB_STANDARD);
      pt.x = (long)(x + 8); pt.y = (long)(y + dy + 1);
      GpiCharStringAt(hps, &pt, (LONG)strlen(name), name);
      pt.x = (long)(x + 3); pt.y = (long)(y + 3);
      GpiCharStringAt(hps, &pt, (LONG)strlen(text), text);
      }
VOID enablefns(void)
{
      fnsavail = TRUE;
      WinSendMsg(WinWindowFromID(hwndFrame, FID_MENU)
                , MM_SETITEMATTR
                , MPFROM2SHORT(ID_SEND, TRUE)
                , MPFROM2SHORT(MIA_DISABLED, ~MIA_DISABLED));
      WinSendMsg(WinWindowFromID(hwndFrame, FID_MENU)
                , MM_SETITEMATTR
                , MPFROM2SHORT(ID_RETRIEVE, TRUE)
                , MPFROM2SHORT(MIA_DISABLED, ~MIA_DISABLED));
      WinSendMsg(WinWindowFromID(hwndFrame, FID_MENU)
                , MM_SETITEMATTR
                , MPFROM2SHORT(ID_EXIT, TRUE)
                , MPFROM2SHORT(MIA_DISABLED, ~MIA_DISABLED));

      }

VOID disablefns(void)
{
      fnsavail = FALSE;
      WinSendMsg(WinWindowFromID(hwndFrame, FID_MENU)
                , MM_SETITEMATTR
                , MPFROM2SHORT(ID_SEND, TRUE)
                , MPFROM2SHORT(MIA_DISABLED, MIA_DISABLED));
      WinSendMsg(WinWindowFromID(hwndFrame, FID_MENU)
                , MM_SETITEMATTR
                , MPFROM2SHORT(ID_RETRIEVE, TRUE)
                , MPFROM2SHORT(MIA_DISABLED, MIA_DISABLED));
      WinSendMsg(WinWindowFromID(hwndFrame, FID_MENU)
                , MM_SETITEMATTR
                , MPFROM2SHORT(ID_EXIT, TRUE)
                , MPFROM2SHORT(MIA_DISABLED, MIA_DISABLED));

      }

void
waitmsgon(void)
{
      ULONG      flCreate;
```

```
        disablefns();
        WinRegisterClass(         // Register window class
                hab,              // Anchor block handle
                "SubWindow",      // Window class name
                SubWindowProc,    // Address of window procedure
                OL,               // No special Class Style
                0                 // No extra window words
                );

        flCreate = FCF_DLGBORDER;     // Set Frame Control Flag

        hwndSubFrame = WinCreateStdWindow(
                hwndFrame,                // Desktop window is parent
                OL,                       // No Class Style
                (PULONG)&flCreate,        // Frame control flag
                "SubWindow",              // Client window class name
                "",                       // No window text
                OL,                       // No special class style
                NULL,                     // Resource is in .EXE file
                ID_WINDOW,                // Frame window identifier
                (PHWND)&hwndSubClient     // Client window handle
                );

        WinSetWindowPos(hwndSubFrame,     // Set the size and position of
                hwndFrame,                // the window before showing.
                100, 100, 225, 50
                SWP_SIZE | SWP_MOVE | SWP_ACTIVATE | SWP_SHOW
                );
        }

void
waitmsgoff(void)
{
        WinDestroyWindow(hwndSubFrame); //Tidy up...
        enablefns();
        }
/******************** Start of window procedure ********************/
MRESULT EXPENTRY SubWindowProc(HWND hwnd, USHORT msg, MPARAM mpl, MPARAM mp2)
{
        HPS   hps;          // Presentation Space handle
        RECTL rc;           // Rectangle coordinates
        POINTL pt;          // String screen coordinates

        switch( msg )
        {
        case WM_PAINT:
                hps = WinBeginPaint(hwnd, NULL, &rc);
                WinFillRect(hps, (PRECTL)&rc, SYSCLR_WINDOW);
                pt.x = 5L; pt.y = 10L;         // Set the text coordinates,
                WinLoadString(hab, NULL, IDS_WAIT, sizeof(message), (PSZ)message);
                GpiCharStringAt(hps, &pt, (long)strlen(message), (PSZ)message);
                WinEndPaint(hps);
                break;
```

```
        default:
            return WinDefWindowProc(hwnd, msg, mpl, mp2);
            }
    return FALSE;
    }
```

A.2 PMAPPC.C

This is the background communications thread of the OS/2 requestor.

```
/*
 * the user transaction program that talks to the two CICS transactions
 *        LSUB and LRET.
 */

#include <os2.h>
#include <string.h>
#include <stdlib.h>
#include <stddef.h>
#include "pmsamp.h"
#include "record.h"
#include <appc.h>

HSEM pascal hsemThreadSem;
extern HWND pascal hwndFrame;
void far pascal appcjob(void);

static char    LocalTPName[] =    "LU62PC";
#define   LocalTPNameLen        (sizeof("LU62PC")-1)
static char    SubmitTPName[] =   "LSUB";
#define   SubmitTPNameLen       (sizeof("LSUB")-1)
static char    RequestTPName[] =  "LRET";
#define   RequestTPNameLen      (sizeof("LRET")-1)
static char    ModeName[] =       "LU62SYS1";
#define   ModeNameLen           (sizeof("LU62SYS1")-1)
static char    LocalLUAlias[] = "PCLU62 ";
#define   LocalLUAliasLen       (sizeof("PCLU62 ")-1)
static char    PartnerLUAlias[] = "CICSLU62";
#define   PartnerLUAliasLen     (sizeof("CICSLU62")-1)
static char    tp_id[8]
long      conv_id;
static int     init(void);

static int     submit(void);
static int     submitappc(void);
static int     request(void);
static void    decodereply(void);
int pascal checkreply(void);
static int     requestappc(void);
static void    request2appc(int type);
int extract(char *d, char *s, int l);
```

```
struct {
     char       name[63];
     char       address[3][63];
     char       postcode[31];
     char       country[15];
          } cics_record;
short     buflen;
void far pascal
appcjob(void)
{
          int ret;
          if (ret = init())
          {
              switch (ret)
              {
          case SV_COMM_SUBSYSTEM_NOT_LOADED:
              WinPostMsg(hwndFrame, NO_COMMS, (MPARAM)0,0);
              DosExit( EXIT_THREAD, 0 );
              }
          }
     while(1)
     {
          DosSemSetWait(hsemThreadSem, -1);
          switch (record.cmd)
          {
          'case      ID_SEND:
              record.rc = submit();
              break;

          case       ID_RETRIEVE:
              record.rc = request();
              break;

          case       ID_EXIT:
              APPC_tp_ended(tp_id);
              DosExit(EXIT_THREAD,0);
              }
          if(record.rc == CICS_ERROR_MESSAGE)
          {
              ret = convert(SV_EBCDIC_TO_ASCII, SV_G, buflen,
                                   record.message, record.message);
              record.message[buflen] = 0;
              }

          WinPostMsg(hwndFrame, DONE, (MPARAM)0, 0);
          }
     }

static int
init(void)
{
     short ret;
```

```
    ret = convert(SV_ASCII_TO_EBCDIC, SV_A,
                    LocalTP NameLen, LocalTPName, LocalTPName);
    if (ret)
        return(ret);
    convert(SV_ASCII_TO_EBCDIC, SV_A,
                    SubmitTPNameLen, SubmitTPName, SubmitTPName);
    convert(SV_ASCII_TO_EBCDIC, SV_A,
                    RequestTPNameLen, RequestTPName, RequestTPName);
    convert (SV_ASCII_TO_EBCDIC, SV_A, ModeNameLen, ModeName, ModeName);
    ret = APPC_tp_started(LocalLUAlias, LocalTpName, LocalTPNameLen, tp_id);
    if (ret != AP_OK)
        return(ret);
    return 0;
    }

static int
submit(void)
{
    // construct cics version of records
    memset((char *)&cics_record, ' ', sizeof(cics_record));
    memcpy(cics_record.name, record.name, strlen(record.name));
    memcpy(cics_record.address[0], record.address[0],
                    strlen(record.address[0]));
    memcpy(cics_record.address[1], record.address[1],
                    strlen(record.address[1]));
    memcpy(cics_record.address[2], record.address[2],
                    strlen(record.address[2]));
    memcpy(cics_record.postcode, record.postcode, strlen(record.postcode));
    memcpy(cics_record.country, record.country, strlen(record.country));
    convert(SV_ASCII_TO_EBCDIC, SV_G, sizeof(cics_record)
                    (char *)&cics_record, (char *)&cics_record);
    return submitappc();
    }

static int
submitappc(void)
{
    short    ret;
    long     lret;
    short    rts;
    short    what;
    short    len;
    ret = APPC_MC_allocate(tp_id,
                    PartnerLUAlias,
                    ModeName,
                    SubmitTPName,
                    SubmitTPNameLen,
                    AP_WHEN_SESSION_ALLOCATED,
                    AP_CONFIRM_SYNC_LEVEL,
                    AP_NONE,
                    NULL, 0,
                    NULL, 0,
```

```
                              &conv_id,
                              &lret);
            if (ret != AP_OK)
            {
                    return RESOURCE_FAILURE;
                    }

            ret = APPC_MC_send_data(tp_id, conv_id, sizeof(cics_record),
                                              (char *)&cics_record, &rts, &lret);
            if (ret != AP_OK)
            {
//          The only thing that can have gone wrong is a resource failure,
//          so there is little point in looking at the return code too much

                    APPC_MC_deallocate(tp_id, conv_id, AP_ABEND, &lret);
                    return RESOURCE_FAILURE;
                    }

            ret = APPC_MC_deallocate(tp_id, conv_id, AP_SYNC_LEVEL, &lret);
            if (ret == AP_OK)
                    return OK;
            else if (ret == AP_DEALLOC_ABEND)
                    return CICS_ABENDED;
            else if (ret != AP_PROG_ERROR_PURGING)
                    return RESOURCE_FAILURE;

//    So now we know that the CICS TP did an ISSUE ERROR.
//    We are now in receive state, and are expecting an
//    error message.

            ret = APPC_MC_receive_and_wait(tp_id, conv_id, record.message,
                          sizeof(record.message)-1, &buflen, &what, &rts, &lret);
            if ((ret == AP_OK) && (what == AP_DATA_COMPLETE))
            {
                    ret = APPC_MC_receive_and_wait(tp_id, conv_id, NULL,
                                          0, &len, &what, &rts, &lret);
                    if (ret != AP_DEALLOC_NORMAL)

//            Something unexpected happened. We already have the error message
//            so we abend the conversation and carry on as if nothing had
//            happened
                            APPC_MC_deallocate(tp_id, conv_id, AP_ABEND, &lret);
                    return CICS_ERROR_MESSAGE;
                    }
            if (ret == AP_DEALLOC_ABEND)
                    return CICS_ABENDED;
            return RESOURCE_FAILURE;
            }

static int
request(void)
{
```

```
        int ret;
        // construct cics version of record
        memset(cics_record.name, ' ', sizeof(cics_record.name));
        memcpy(cics_record.name, record.name, strlen(record.name));
        convert(SV_ASCII_TO_EBCDIC, SV_G, sizeof(cics_record.name),
                                    cics_record.name, cics_record.name);
        switch(ret = requestappc())
        {
        case OK:
                break;

        case DONE_BUT:
                break;

        case RESOURCE_FAILURE:
                break;

        case CICS_ABENDED:
                break;

        case CICS_ERROR_MESSAGE:
                break;
                }
        if (ret != OK)
                return ret;
        decodereply();
        if ((ret = checkreply()) == OK)
        {
                request2appc(OK);
                }
        else
        {
                request2appc(NOT_OK);
                }
        return ret;
        }

static void
decodereply(void)
{
        convert(SV_EBCDIC_TO_ASCII, SV_G, sizeof(cics_record),
                            (char *)&cics_record, (char *)&cics_record);
        extract(record.address[0], cics_record.address[0],
                                    sizeof(cics_record.address[0]));
        extract(record.address[1], cics_record.address[1],
                                    sizeof(cics_record.address[1]));
        extract(record.address[2], cics_record.address[2],
                                    sizeof(cics_record.address[2]));
        extract(record.postcode, cics_record.postcode,
                                    sizeof(cics_record.postcode));
        extract(record.country, cics_record.country, sizeof(cics_record.country));
}
```

```
static int
requestappc(void)
{
    short    ret;
    long     lret;
    short    rts;
    short    what;
    short    len;
    ret = APPC_MC_allocate(tp_id,
                    PartnerLUAlias,
                    ModeName,
                    RequestTPName,
                    RequestTPNameLen,
                    AP_WHEN_SESSION_ALLOCATED,
                    AP_CONFIRM_SYNC_LEVEL,
                    AP_NONE,
                    NULL, 0,
                    NULL, 0,

                    &conv_id,
                    &lret);
    if (ret != AP_OK)
    {
        return RESOURCE_FAILURE;
    }
    ret = APPC_MC_send_data(tp_id, conv_id, sizeof(cics_record.name),
                                    cics_record.name, &rts, &lret);
    if (ret != AP_OK)
    {

//      The only thing that can have gone wrong is a resource failure,
//      so there is little point in looking at the return code too much

        APPC_MC_deallocate(tp_id, conv_id, AP_ABEND, &lret);
        return RESOURCE_FAILURE;
    }

    ret = APPC_MC_receive_and_wait(tp_id, conv_id, (char *)&cics_record,
                        sizeof(cics_record), &buflen, &what, &rts, &lret);
    if (ret == AP_DEALLOC_ABEND)
        return CICS_ABENDED;
    else if (ret == AP_PROG_ERROR_PURGING)
    {
//      So now we know that the CICS TP did an ISSUE ERROR.
//      We are now in receive state, and are expecting an
//      error message

        ret = APPC_MC_receive_and_wait(tp_id, conv_id, record.message,
                        sizeof(record.message)-1, &buflen, &what, &rts, &lret);
        if ((ret == AP_OK) || (What == AP_DATA_COMPLETE))
        {
            ret = APPC_MC_receive_and_wait(tp_id, conv_id, NULL, 0, &len,
                                    what, &rts, &lret);
```

```
                     if (ret != AP_DEALLOC_NORMAL)
//                           Something unexpected happened. We already have the error
//                           message so we abend the conversation and carry on as if
//                           nothing had happened
                             APPC_MC_deallocate(tp_id, conv_id, AP_ABEND, &lret);
                     return CICS_ERROR_MESSAGE;
                     }
             if (ret == AP_DEALLOC_ABEND)
                     return CICS_ABENDED;
             return RESOURCE_FAILURE;
             }
        else if (ret != AP_OK)
             return RESOURCE_FAILURE;

//   We now have the reply from CICS. We need to issue a receive&wait
//   to get the confirm_deallocate then we have to return to the processing
//   routine for it to check the data before we can continue

        ret = APPC_MC_receive_and_wait(tp_id, conv_id, NULL, 0,
                                       &len, &what, &rts, &lret);
        if ((ret != AP_OK) || (what != AP_CONFIRM_DEALLOCATE))
//           Well we have the data but we do not seem to have the confirm deallocate
//           We may as well use the data, but...

             return DONE_BUT;
        return OK;
        }

static void
request2appc(int type)
{
        long      lret;
        short     rts;

        if (type == OK)
        {
             APPC_MC_confirmed(tp_id, conv_id, &lret);
             return;
             }
//   There is little point in checking the return codes from these
//   verbs: if the conversation has failed, or the remote TP has
//   abended then the verbs fail. So what?
        APPC_MC_send_error(tp_id, conv_id, 0, &lret);
        convert(SV_ASCII_TO_EBCDIC, SV_G, buflen, record.message, record.message);
        APPC_MC_send_data(tp_id, conv_id, buflen, record.message, &rts, &lret);
        APPC_MC_deallocate(tp_id, conv_id, AP_FLUSH, &LRET);
        }

int extract(char *d, char *s, int l)
{
```

```
    memset(d, '\0', l + 1);
    /* get the deblanked length */
    while(l)
    {
        if(s[l-1] > ' '
            break;
        else
            l--;
    }
    if(l > 0)
        memcpy(d, s, l);
    return l;
    }
int pascal checkreply(void)
{
    if (record.name[1] == 'X')
    {
        strcpy(record.message, "RECORD REJECTED BY PC PROGRAM");
        return NOT_OK;
}
    return OK;
    }
```

A.3 PMSAMP.RC

This is the presentation manager resource file for the C program.

```
#define  INCL_PM
#include <os2.h>
#include "pmsamp.h"

MENU ID_PMSAMP   PRELOAD
BEGIN
    MENUITEM    "~Send"                 ,  ID_SEND
    MENUITEM    "~Retrieve"             ,  ID_RETRIEVE
    MENUITEM    "~About"                ,  ID_ABOUT
    MENUITEM    "~Help"                 ,  ID_HELP
    MENUITEM    "E~xit"                 ,  ID_EXIT
END

ICON    ID_PMSAMP pmsamp.ico

ACCELTABLE ID_PMSAMP   PRELOAD
BEGIN

    VK_F3       ,  IDA_EXIT      ,  VIRTUALKEY
END

STRINGTABLE PRELOAD
BEGIN
    IDS_NAME        ,    "Name"
    IDS_ADDRESS     ,    "Address"
```

```
IDS_POSTCODE      ,    "Post Code"
IDS_COUNTRY       ,    "Country"
IDS_EXIT          ,    "Do you really want to quit?"
IDS_ABOUT         ,    "A simple presentation manager program
                       using a separate thread to communicate
                       with CICS transactions using APPC"
IDS_RESOURCEFAIL, "Failed to connect with TP, or link failed"
IDS_CICSABEND     ,    "CICS TP abended"
IDS_DONE_BUT      ,    "CICS TP abended after data returned"
IDS_WAIT          ,    "Waiting for response from CICS TP"
IDS_NO_COMMS      ,    "Communications manager not loaded"
IDS_NOT_OK        ,    "We rejected the reply from CICS"
IDS_HELP          ,    "Presentation manager APPC example
                       Select SEND to send a record to
                       a CICS transaction program.
                       Select RETRIEVE to retrieve a
                       record from a different CICS
                       transaction program."
END
DLGTEMPLATE DLG_SEND LOADONCALL MOVEABLE DISCARDABLE
BEGIN
    DIALOG "Send a Record", DLG_SEND, 7, 6, 200, 140, FS_NOBYTEALIGN |
                                                        FS_DLGBORDER |
            WS_VISIBLE | WS_CLIPSIBLINGS | WS_SAVEBITS,
        FCF_DLGBORDER || FCF_NOBYTEALIGN || FCF_TITLEBAR
    BEGIN
        CONTROL "Name", 1,      18, 98, 184, 18, WC_STATIC,
                SS_GROUPBOX | WS_GROUP | WS_VISIBLE
        CONTROL ""          DLG_NAME, 20, 100, 180, 8,  WC_ENTRYFIELD,
                ES_LEFT | WS_TABSTOP | WS_VISIBLE | ES_AUTOSCROLL
        CONTROL "Address".          1,     18, 58, 184, 38, WC_STATIC,
                SS_GROUPBOX | WS_GROUP | WS_VISIBLE
        CONTROL "",         DLG_ADDRESS1,    20, 80, 180, 8,   WC_ENTRYFIELD,
                ES_LEFT | WS_TABSTOP | WS_VISIBLE | ES_AUTOSCROLL
        CONTROL "",         DLG_ADDRESS2,    20, 70, 180, 8,   WC_ENTRYFIELD,
                ES_LEFT | WS_TABSTOP | WS_VISIBLE | ES_AUTOSCROLL
        CONTROL "",         DLG_ADDRESS3,    20, 60, 180, 8,   WC_ENTRYFIELD,
                ES_LEFT | WS_TABSTOP | WS_VISIBLE | ES_AUTOSCROLL
        CONTROL "Post Code",      1,      18, 38, 70, 18, WC_STATIC,
                SS_GROUPBOX | WS_GROUP | WS_VISIBLE
        CONTROL "",         DLG_POSTCODE, 20, 40, 66, 8,  WC_ENTRYFIELD,
                ES_LEFT | WS_TABSTOP | WS_VISIBLE | ES_AUTOSCROLL
        CONTROL "Country",        1,      18, 18, 184, 18, WC_STATIC,
                SS_GROUPBOX | WS_GROUP | WS_VISIBLE
        CONTROL "",         DLG_COUNTRY,  20, 20, 180, 8,  WC_ENTRYFIELD,
                ES_LEFT | WS_TABSTOP | WS_VISIBLE | ES_AUTOSCROLL
        CONTROL "Enter", 1,            6, 4, 40, 12,  WC_BUTTON
                BS_PUSHBUTTON | BS_DEFAULT | WS_GROUP | WS_TABSTOP | WS_VISIBLE
        CONTROL "Cancel", 2,          60, 4, 40, 12,  WC_BUTTON
                BS_PUSHBUTTON | WS_VISIBLE
    END
END
```

```
DLGTEMPLATE DLG_RETRIEVE LOADONCALL MOVEABLE DISCARDABLE
BEGIN
     DIALOG "Retrieve a Record", DLG_RETRIEVE, 7, 6, 200, 60, FS_NOBYTEALIGN |
                                                       FS_DLGBORDER |
               WS_VISIBLE | WS_CLIPSIBLINGS | WS_SAVEBITS,
            FCF_DLGBORDER || FCF_NOBYTEALIGN || FCF_TITLEBAR
       BEGIN
            CONTROL "Name", 1,      18, 18, 184, 18, WC_STATIC,
                 SS_GROUPBOX | WS_GROUP | WS_VISIBLE
            CONTROL ""       DLG_NAME, 20, 20, 180, 8,  WC_ENTRYFIELD,
                 ES_LEFT | WS_TABSTOP | WS_VISIBLE | ES_AUTOSCROLL
            CONTROL "Enter",  1,         6, 4, 40, 12,    WC_BUTTON
                 BS_PUSHBUTTON | BS_DEFAULT | WS_GROUP | WS_TABSTOP | WS_VISIBLE
            CONTROL "Cancel", 2,        60, 4, 40, 12,    WC_BUTTON
                 BS_PUSHBUTTON | BS_VISIBLE
       END
     END
END
```

A.4   LU62SUB.COB   This is the CICS TP which accepts and confirms or rejects a record.

```
ID DIVISION                                                  REC00010
PROGRAM-ID                      LU62SUB                       REC00020
ENVIRONMENT DIVISION                                          REC00030
DATA DIVISION                                                 REC00040
WORKING-STORAGE SECTION.                                      REC00050
01  BUF                                                       REC00060
    02  FIRST-CHAR          PIC X(1).                         REC00070
    02  REST                PIC X(511).                       REC00080
77  BUF-LEN                 PIC S9(4) COMP.                   REC00090
77  ERROR-MSG               PIC X(29)                         REC00100
          VALUE IS 'MESSAGE MUST NOT START WITH X'.           REC00110
77  ERROR-MSG-LEN           PIC S9(4) COMP                    REC00120
          VALUE IS 29.                                        REC00130
PROCEDURE DIVISION.                                           REC00140
START-RECVLU62                                                REC00150
    MOVE 512 TO BUF-LEN.                                      REC00160
    EXEC CICS     RECEIVE                                     REC00170
                  INTO(BUF)                                   REC00180
                  LENGTH(BUF-LEN)                             REC00190
                  END-EXEC.                                   REC00200
    IF  FIRST-CHAR = 'X'                                      REC00210
        GO TO NO-GOOD.                                        REC00220
    EXEC CICS ISSUE CONFIRMATION END-EXEC.                    REC00230
    EXEC CICS FREE END-EXEC.                                  REC00240
    EXEC CICS RETURN END-EXEC.                                REC00250
    GOBACK.                                                   REC00260
                                                              REC00270
```

```
NO-GOOD.                                                  REC00280
    EXEC CICS ISSUE ERROR END-EXEC.                      REC00290
    EXEC CICS        SEND                                 REC00300
                     FROM(ERROR-MSG)                      REC00310
                     LENGTH(ERROR-MSG-LEN)                REC00320
                     END-EXEC.                            REC00330
    EXEC CICS SEND LAST WAIT END-EXEC.                    REC00340
    EXEC CICS FREE END-EXEC.                              REC00350
    EXEC CICS RETURN END-EXEC.                            REC00360
    GOBACK.                                               REC00370
```

A.5 LU62RET.COB   This is the CICS TP that takes a command, either accepts and replies to it, or rejects it.

```
ID DIVISION.                                              REC00010
PROGRAM-ID.                      LU62RET.                 REC00020
ENVIRONMENT DIVISION.                                     REC00030
DATA DIVISION.                                            REC00040
WORKING-STORAGE SECTION.                                  REC00050
01  BUF                                                   REC00060
    02  FIRST-CHAR           PIC X(1).                    REC00070
    02  REST                 PIC X(511).                  REC00080
77  BUF-LEN                  PIC S9(4) COMP.              REC00090
77  ERROR-MSG                PIC X(29)                    REC00100
            VALUE IS 'MESSAGE MUST NOT START WITH X'.     REC00110
77  ERROR-MSG-LEN            PIC S9(4) COMP               REC00120
                VALUE IS 29.                              REC00130
PROCEDURE DIVISION.                                       REC00140
START-LU62RET.                                            REC00150
*                                                         REC00160
*    1.  WE GET THE COMMAND                               REC00170
*                                                         REC00180
    MOVE 512 TO BUF-LEN.                                  REC00190
    EXEC CICS        RECEIVE                              REC00200
                     INTO(BUF)                            REC00210
                     LENGTH(BUF-LEN)                      REC00220
                     END-EXEC.                            REC00230
    IF  FIRST-CHAR = 'X'                                  REC00240
        GO TO NO-GOOD.                                    REC00250
*                                                         REC00260
*    2.  WE SEND THE REPLY AND ASK FOR CONFIRMATION       REC00270
*                                                         REC00280
    EXEC CICS        SEND                                 REC00290
                     FROM(BUF)                            REC00300
                     LENGTH(BUF-LEN)                      REC00310
                     END-EXEC.                            REC00320
```

```
        EXEC CICS SEND LAST CONFIRM END-EXEC.              REC00330
        IF  EIBERR NOT = LOW-VALUE                         REC00340
            GO TO NO-CONF.                                 REC00350
        EXEC CICS FREE END-EXEC.                           REC00360
        EXEC CICS RETURN END-EXEC.                         REC00370
        GOBACK.                                            REC00380
 *                                                         REC00390
 NO-CONF.                                                  REC00400
 *                                                         REC00410
 *    3.  WE GET THE ERROR MESSAGE                         REC00420
 *                                                         REC00430
        MOVE 512 TO BUF-LEN.                               REC00440
        EXEC CICS       RECEIVE                            REC00450
                        INTO(BUF)                          REC00460
                        LENGTH(BUF-LEN)                    REC00470
                        END-EXEC.                          REC00480
        EXEC CICS       WRITEQ                             REC00490
                        TS                                 REC00500
                        QUEUE('LU62SUBQ')                  REC00510
                        FROM(BUF)                          REC00520
                        LENGTH(BUF-LEN)                    REC00530
                        END-EXEC.                          REC00540
 *                                                         REC00550
 *    4.  WE ARE CONFIDENT THAT EIBFREE WAS SET.           REC00560
 *                                                         REC00570
        EXEC CICS FREE END-EXEC.                           REC00580
        EXEC CICS RETURN END-EXEC.                         REC00590
        GOBACK.                                            REC00600
 *                                                         REC00610
 NO-GOOD.                                                  REC00620
 *                                                         REC00630
 *    2E. WE ISSUE AN ERROR BEFORE SENDING ERROR MESSAGE.  REC00640
 *                                                         REC00650
        EXEC CICS ISSUE ERROR END-EXEC.                    REC00660
 *                                                         REC00670
 *    3E. SEND THE ERROR MESSAGE.                          REC00680
 *                                                         REC00690
        EXEC CICS       SEND                               REC00700
                        FROM(ERROR-MSG)                    REC00710
                        LENGTH(ERROR-MSG-LEN)              REC00720
                        END-EXEC.                          REC00730
 *                                                         REC00740
 *    4E. DEALLOCATE THE CONVERSATION.                     REC00750
 *                                                         REC00760
        EXEC CICS SEND LAST WAIT END-EXEC.                 REC00770
        EXEC CICS FREE END-EXEC.                           REC00780
        EXEC CICS RETURN END-EXEC.                         REC00790
        GOBACK.                                            REC00800
```

A.6 LU62SUB,
VM/CMS version

This is the VM/CMS CPI-C program that receives a record and either confirms or rejects it.

```
ID DIVISION.                                                   LU600010
PROGRAM-ID.                    LU62SUBV.                       LU600020
ENVIRONMENT DIVISION.                                         LU600030
DATA DIVISION.                                                LU600040
WORKING-STORAGE SECTION.                                      LU600050
01  BUF.                                                      LU600060
    03  FIRST-CHAR            PIC X(1).                       LU600070
    03  REST                  PIC X(511).                     LU600080
77  BUF-LEN                   PIC S9(9) COMP.                 LU600090
77  ERROR-MSG                 PIC X(29)                       LU600100
          VALUE IS 'MESSAGE MUST NOT START WITH X'.           LU600110
77  ERROR-MSG-LEN             PIC S9(9) COMP                  LU600120
          VALUE IS +29.                                       LU600130
*                                                             LU600140
* CPI-COMMUNICATIONS PSEUDONYM COPY BOOK                      LU600150
*                                                             LU600160
    COPY CMCOBOL.                                             LU600170
*                                                             LU600180
* CPI-COMMUNICATIONS PSEUDONYM COPY BOOK FOR VM/SP  ADD-ONS.  (DGA)   LU600190
*                                                             LU600200
    COPY CMCOBOLX.                                            LU600210
PROCEDURE DIVISION.                                           LU600220
START-LU62SUBV.                                               LU600230
* IDENTIFY OURSELVES TO VM FIRST AS A GLOBAL RESOURCE         LU600240
    MOVE 'LSUB' TO RESOURCE-ID.                               LU600250
    MOVE 2 TO RESOURCE-MANAGER-TYPE.                          LU600260
    MOVE 1 TO SERVICE-MODE.                                   LU600270
    MOVE 1 TO SECURITY-LEVEL-FLAG.                            LU600280
    CALL 'XCIDRM' USING RESOURCE-ID                           LU600290
                    RESOURCE-MANAGER-TYPE                     LU600300
                    SEVICE-MODE                               LU600310
                    SECURITY-LEVEL-FLAG                       LU600320
                    CM-RETCODE.                               LU600330
    IF  CM-OK                                                 LU600340
        DISPLAY 'LU62SUBV RESOURCE LSUB IDENTIFIED TO VM'     LU600350
    ELSE                                                      LU600360
        DISPLAY 'LU62SUBV UNABLE TO ATTACH TO VM'             LU600370
        STOP RUN.                                             LU600380
    CALL 'XCWOE' USING RESOURCE-ID                            LU600390
                    CONVERSATION-ID                           LU600400
                    EVENT-TYPE                                LU600410
                    DATA-LENGTH                               LU600420
                    CONSOLE-INPUT-BUFFER                      LU600430
                    CM-RETCODE.                               LU600440
    IF  CM-OK                                                 LU600450
        NEXT SENTENCE                                         LU600460
    ELSE                                                      LU600470
        DISPLAY 'LU62SUBV ERROR WITH WAIT-ON-EVENT', CM-RETCODE  LU600480
        GO TO END-LU62SUBV.                                   LU600490
```

```
        IF  XC-ALLOCATION-REQUEST                               LU600500
            NEXT SENTENCE                                       LU600510
        ELSE                                                    LU600520
            DISPLAY 'LU62SUBV WAIT ON EVENT TYPE', EVENT-TYPE   LU600530
            GO TO END-LU62SUBV.                                 LU600540
*                                                               LU600550
        CALL 'CMACCP' USING CONVERSATION-ID                     LU600560
                            CM-RETCODE.                         LU600570
        IF  CM-OK                                               LU600580
            DISPLAY 'LU62SUBV CONVERSATION ALLOCATED'           LU600590
        ELSE                                                    LU600600
            DISPLAY 'LU62SUBV UNABLE TO ALLOCATE CONVERSATION'  LU600610
            GO TO END-LU62SUBV.                                 LU600620
        MOVE 512 TO BUF-LEN.                                    LU600630
        CALL 'CMRCV' USING CONVERSATION-ID                      LU600640
                            BUF                                 LU600650
                            BUF-LEN                             LU600660
                            DATA-RECEIVED                       LU600670
                            BUF-LEN                             LU600680
                            STATUS-RECEIVED                     LU600690
                            REQUEST-TO-SEND-RECEIVED            LU600700
                            CM-RETCODE.                         LU600710
        IF  FIRST-CHAR = 'X'                                    LU600720
            GO TO NO-GOOD.                                      LU600730
        CALL 'CMCFMD' USING CONVERSATION-ID                     LU600740
                            CM-RETCODE.                         LU600750
        DISPLAY 'LU62SUBV COMPLETE OK'.                         LU600760
* REMOVE OURSELVES FROM VM                                      LU600770
END-LU62SUBV.                                                   LU600780
        CALL 'XCTRRM' USING RESOURCE-ID                         LU600790
                            CM-RETCODE.                         LU600800
        STOP RUN.                                               LU600810
                                                                LU600820
NO-GOOD.                                                        LU600830
        CALL 'CMSERR' USING CONVERSATION-ID                     LU600840
                            REQUEST-TO-SEND-RECEIVED            LU600850
                            CM-RETCODE.                         LU600860
        CALL 'CMSEND' USING CONVERSATION-ID                     LU600870
                            ERROR-MSG                           LU600880
                            ERROR-MSG-LEN                       LU600890
                            REQUEST-TO-SEND-RECEIVED            LU600900
                            CM-RETCODE.                         LU600910
        MOVE 1 TO DEALLOCATE-TYPE.                              LU600920
        CALL.'CMSDT' USING CONVERSATION-ID                      LU600930
                            DEALLOCATE-TYPE                     LU600940
                            CM-RETCODE.                         LU600950
        CALL 'CMDEAL' USING CONVERSATION-ID                     LU600960
                            CM-RETCODE.                         LU600970
        DISPLAY 'LU62SUBV NO GOOD'.                             LU600980
* REMOVE OURSELVES FROM VM                                      LU600990
        CALL 'XCTRRM' USING RESOURCE-ID                         LU601000
                            CM-RETCODE.                         LU601010
        STOP RUN.                                               LU601020
```

A.7 LU62RET, VM/CMS version

This is the VM/CMS CPI-C program that takes a request and either replies to it or rejects it.

```
ID DIVISION                                                    LU600010
PROGRAM-ID.                      LU62RETV.                     LU600020
ENVIRONMENT DIVISION.                                          LU600030
DATA DIVISION.                                                 LU600040
WORKING-STORAGE SECTION.                                       LU600050
01  BUF.                                                       LU600060
    03  FIRST-CHAR             PIC X(1).                       LU600070
    03  REST                   PIC X(511).                     LU600080
77  BUF-LEN                    PIC S9(9) COMP.                 LU600090
77  ERROR-MSG                  PIC X(29)                       LU600100
             VALUE IS 'MESSAGE MUST NOT START WITH X'.         LU600110
77  ERROR-MSG-LEN             PIC S9(9) COMP                   LU600120
             VALUE IS +29.                                     LU600130
*                                                              LU600140
* CPI-COMMUNICATIONS PSEUDONYM COPY BOOK                       LU600150
*                                                              LU600160
    COPY CMCOBOL.                                              LU600170
*                                                              LU600180
* CPI-COMMUNICATIONS PSEUDONYM COPY BOOK FOR VM/SP ADD-ONS. (DGA)  LU600190
*                                                              LU600200
    COPY CMCOBOLX.                                             LU600210
PROCEDURE DIVISION.                                            LU600220
START-LU62RETV.                                                LU600230
*                                                              LU600240
* IDENTIFY OURSELVES TO VM FIRST AS A GLOBAL RESOURCE          LU600250
*                                                              LU600260
    MOVE 'LRET' TO RESOURCE-ID.                                LU600270
    MOVE 2 TO RESOURCE-MANAGER-TYPE.                           LU600280
    MOVE 1 TO SERVICE-MODE.                                    LU600290
    MOVE 1 TO SECURITY-LEVEL-FLAG.                             LU600300
    CALL 'XCIDRM' USING RESOURCE-ID                            LU600310
                        RESOURCE-MANAGER-TYPE                  LU600320
                        SERVICE-MODE                           LU600330
                        SECURITY-LEVEL-FLAG                    LU600340
                        CM-RETCODE.                            LU600350
    IF  CM-OK                                                  LU600360
        DISPLAY 'LU62RETV RESOURCE LRET IDENTIFIED TO VM'      LU600370
    ELSE                                                       LU600380
        DISPLAY 'LU62RETV UNABLE TO ATTACH TO VM'              LU600390
        STOP RUN.                                              LU600400
    CALL 'XCWOE' USING RESOURCE-ID                             LU600410
                       CONVERSATION-ID                         LU600420
                       EVENT-TYPE                              LU600430
                       DATA-LENGTH                             LU600440
                       CONSOLE-INPUT-BUFFER                    LU600450
                       CM-RETCODE.                             LU600460
    IF  CM-OK                                                  LU600470
        NEXT SENTENCE                                          LU600480
    ELSE                                                       LU600490
```

```
        DISPLAY 'LU62RETV WAIT-ON-EVENT ERROR ', CM-RETCODE          LU600500
        GO TO END-LU62RETV.                                          LU600510
    IF  XC-ALLOCATION-REQUEST                                        LU600520
        NEXT SENTENCE                                                LU600530
    ELSE                                                             LU600540
        DISPLAY 'LU62RETV WAIT ON EVENT TYPE', EVENT-TYPE            LU600550
        GO TO END-LU62RETV.                                          LU600560
*                                                                    LU600570
    CALL 'CMACCP' USING CONVERSATION-ID                              LU600580
                    CM-RETCODE.                                      LU600590
    IF  CM-OK                                                        LU500600
        DISPLAY 'LU62RETV CONVERSATION ALLOCATED'                    LU600610
    ELSE                                                             LU600620
        DISPLAY 'LU62RETV UNABLE TO ALLOCATE CONVERSATION'           LU600630
        GO TO END-LU62RETV.                                          LU600640
*                                                                    LU600650
* 1. WE GET THE COMMAND                                              LU600660
*                                                                    LU600670
    MOVE 512 TO BUF-LEN.                                             LU600680
    CALL 'CMRCV' USING CONVERSATION-ID                               LU600690
                    BUF                                              LU600700
                    BUF-LEN                                          LU600710
                    DATA-RECEIVED                                    LU600720
                    BUF-LEN                                          LU600730
                    STATUS-RECEIVED                                  LU600740
                    REQUEST-TO-SEND-RECEIVED                         LU600750
                    CM-RETCODE.                                      LU600760
    IF  FIRST-CHAR = 'X'                                             LU600770
        GO TO NO-GOOD.                                               LU600780
*                                                                    LU600790
* 2. WE SEND THE REPLY AND ASK FOR CONFIRMATION                      LU600800
*                                                                    LU600810
    CALL 'CMSEND' USING CONVERSATION-ID                              LU600820
                    BUF                                              LU600830
                    BUF-LEN                                          LU600840
                    REQUEST-TO-SEND-RECEIVED                         LU600850
                    CM-RETCODE.                                      LU600860
    MOVE O TO DEALLOCATE-TYPE.                                       LU600870
    CALL 'CMSDT' USING CONVERSATION-ID                               LU600880
                    DEALLOCATE-TYPE                                  LU600890
                    CM-RETCODE.                                      LU600900
    CALL 'CMDEAL' USING CONVERSATION-ID                              LU600910
                    CM-RETCODE.                                      LU600920
  IF NOT CM-OK                                                       LU600930
     GO TO NO-CONF.                                                  LU600940
  DISPLAY 'LU62RETV COMPLETE OK'.                                    LU600950
*                                                                    LU600960
* REMOVE OURSELVES FROM VM                                           LU600970
*                                                                    LU600980
  END-LU62RETV.                                                      LU600990
    CALL 'XCTRRM' USING RESOURCE-ID                                  LU601000
                    CM-RETCODE.                                      LU601010
    STOP RUN.                                                        LU601020
```

```
*                                                              LU601030
  NO-CONF                                                      LU601040
*                                                              LU601050
* 3. WE GET THE ERROR MESSAGE                                  LU601060
*                                                              LU601070
    MOVE 512 TO BUF-LEN.                                       LU601080
    CALL 'CMRCV' USING CONVERSATION-ID                         LU601090
                      BUF                                      LU601100
                      BUF-LEN                                  LU601110
                      DATA-RECEIVED                            LU601120
                      BUF-LEN                                  LU601130
                      STATUS-RECEIVED                          LU601140
                      REQUEST-TO-SEND-RECEIVED                 LU601150
                      CM-RETCODE.                              LU601160
    DISPLAY BUF.                                               LU601170
*                                                              LU601180
* 4. WE ARE CONFIDENT THAT RETCODE WAS CM-DEALLOCATED-NORMAL   LU601190
*                                                              LU601200
    CALL 'XCTRRM' USING RESOURCE-ID                            LU601210
                      CM-RETCODE.                              LU601220
    STOP RUN.                                                  LU601230
*                                                              LU601240
  NO-GOOD.                                                     LU601250
*                                                              LU601260
* 2E. WE ISSUE AN ERROR BEFORE SENDING ERROR MESSAGE           LU601270
*                                                              LU601280
    CALL 'CMSERR' USING CONVERSATION-ID                        LU601290
                      REQUEST-TO-SEND-RECEIVED                 LU601300
                      CM-RETCODE.                              LU601310
*                                                              LU601320
* 3E. SEND THE ERROR MESSAGE                                   LU601330
*                                                              LU601340
    CALL 'CMSEND' USING CONVERSATION-ID                        LU601350
                      ERROR-MSG                                LU601360
                      ERROR-MSG-LEN                            LU601370
                      REQUEST-TO-SEND-RECEIVED                 LU601380
                      CM-RETCODE.                              LU601390
*                                                              LU601400
* 4E. DEALLOCATE THE CONVERSATION                              LU601410
*                                                              LU601420
    MOVE 1 TO DEALLOCATE-TYPE.                                 LU601430
    CALL 'CMSDT' USING CONVERSATION-ID                         LU601440
                      DEALLOCATE-TYPE                          LU601450
                      CM-RETCODE.                              LU601460
    CALL 'CMDEAL' USING CONVERSATION-ID                        LU601470
                      CM-RETCODE.                              LU601480
    DISPLAY 'LU62RETV NO GOOD'.                                LU601490
*                                                              LU601500
* REMOVE OURSELVES FROM VM                                     LU601510
*                                                              LU601520
    CALL 'XCTRRM' USING RESOURCE-ID                            LU601530
                      CM-RETCODE.                              LU601540
    STOP RUN.                                                  LU601550
```

Appendix B
APPC Libraries for OS/2

The following C subroutines are used in the sample code in Appendix A, and also by the code fragments in the main text. They show how the actual call provided by the communications manager can be hidden behind a set of subroutines which provide a more usable interface.

The files listed are:

APPC.H	Defines the entry points.
ALLOCATE.C	APPC_allocate and APPC_MC_allocate.
CONFIRM.C	APPC_confirm and APPC_MC_confirm.
CONFIRMD.C	APPC_confirmed and APPC_MC_confirmed.
DEALLOC.C	APPC_deallocate and APPC_MC_deallocate.
RECALLOC.C	APPC_receive_allocate.
RECVWAIT.C	APPC_receive_and_wait and APPC_MC_receive_and_wait.
SEND_ERR.C	APPC_send_error and APPC_MC_send_error.
SENDDATA.C	APPC_send_data and APPC_MC_send_data.
TPSTART.C	APPC_tp_started.
TPENDED.C	APPC_tp_ended.
CONVERT.C	convert.
SHALLOC.H	Defines the shared memory entry points used by the library functions.
SHALLOC.C	shalloc, shfree and fmemcpy.

B.1 APPC.H   This header file contains the function prototypes for the various APPC interface procedures used in the example program and in the examples in the text.

```
#include <appc_c.h>
#include <acssvcc.h>

unsigned short        cdecl        APPC_allocate(char * tp_id,
                char *     partner_lu_name,
                char *     mode_name,
                char *     tpn,
                unsigned short        tpn_len,
                unsigned short        return_control,
                unsigned short        sync_level,
                unsigned short        security,
                char *     password,
                unsigned short        password_len,
                char *     user_id,
                unsigned short        user_id_len,
                long *     conv_id,
                long *     ret2);

unsigned short        cdecl APPC_confirm(char * tp_id,
                long        conv_id,
                unsigned short *    rts,
                long *     ret2);

unsigned short        cdecl APPC_confirmed(char * tp_id,
                long        conv_id,
                long *     ret2);

unsigned short        cdecl APPC_deallocate(char * tp_id,
                long        conv_id,
                unsigned short        type,
                unsigned short        log_data_len,
                char *     log_data,
                long *     ret2);

unsigned short        cdecl APPC_receive_and_wait(char * tp_id,
                long        conv_id,
                char *     data_id,
                unsigned short        max_length,
                unsigned short *    data_length,
                unsigned short *    what_received,
                unsigned short *    rts_received,
                long *     ret2);

unsigned short        cdecl APPC_send_data(char * tp_id,
                long        conv_id,
                unsigned short        data_length,
                char *     data_ptr,
```

```
                         unsigned short *    rts-received,
                         long *    ret2);

unsigned short           cdecl APPC_send_error(char * tp-id,
                         long         conv-id,
                         unsigned short        type,
                         unsigned short        log-data-length,
                         char *    log-data-ptr,
                         unsigned short *    rts-received,
                         long *    ret2);

unsigned short           cdecl       APPC_MC_allocate(char * tp-id,
                 char *    partner-lu-name,
                 char *    mode-name,
                 char *    tpn,
                 unsigned short        tpn-len,
                 unsigned short        return-control,
                 unsigned short        sync-level,
                 unsigned short        security,
                 char *    password,
                 unsigned short        password-len,
                 char *    user-id,
                 unsigned short        user-id-len,
                 long *    conv-id,
                 long *    ret2);

unsigned short           cdecl APPC_MC_confirm(char * tp-id,
                         long         conv-id,
                         unsigned short *    rts,
                         long *    ret2);

unsigned short           cdecl APPC_MC_confirmed(char * tp-id,
                         long         conv-id,
                         long *    ret2);

unsigned short           cdecl APPC_MC_deallocate(char * tp-id,
                         long         conv-id,
                         unsigned short        type,
                         long *    ret2);

unsigned short           cdecl APPC_MC_receive-and_wait(char * tp-id,
                         long         conv-id,
                         char *    data-id,
                         unsigned short        max-length,
                         unsigned short *    data-length,
                         unsigned short *    what-received,
                         unsigned short *    rts-received,
                         long *    ret2);

unsigned short           cdecl APPC_MC_send-data(char * tp-id,
                         long         conv-id,
                         unsigned short        data-length,
```

```
                        char *     data_ptr,
                        unsigned short *   rts_received,
                        long *     ret2);

unsigned short          cdecl APPC_MC_send_error(char * tp_id,
                        long       conv_id,
                        unsigned short *     rts_received,
                        long *     ret2);

unsigned short          cdecl APPC_receive_allocate(char * tp_name,
                        char *     tp_id,
                        long *     conv_id,
                        unsigned short *   sync_level,
                        unsigned short *   conversation_type,
                        char *     user_id,
                        char *     lu_alias,
                        char *     partner_lu_name,
                        char *     mode_name,
                        long *     ret2);

unsigned short          cdecl APPC_tp_started(char * lu_id,
                        char *     tp_name,
                        unsigned short       tp_name_len,
                        char *     tp_id);

unsigned short          cdecl APPC_tp_ended(char * tp_id);

unsigned short
convert(unsigned short          dir,
        unsigned short          type,
        unsigned short          len,
        char *          source,
        char *          target);
```

B.2 ALLOCATE.C

```
#include "appc_c.h"
#include <stdlib.h>
#include <string.h>
static unsigned short
allocate(      unsigned short       conv_type,
        char *     tp_id,
        char *     partner_lu_name,
        char *     mode_name,
        char *     tpn,              unsigned short     tpn_len,
```

```
    unsigned short      return_control,
    unsigned short      sync_level,
    unsigned short      security,
    char *    password,      unsigned short    password_len,
    char *    user_id,       unsigned short    user_id_len,
    long *    conv_id,
    long *    ret2)


{


static struct allocate alloc_rec = {
    AP_M_ALLOCATE,      AP_MAPPED_CONVERSATION,      /* op codes */
    0,                  /* reserved */
    0,          OL,                              /* return codes*/
    "",                 /* TP_ID */
    OL,                 /* conversation id*/
    AP_MAPPED_CONVERSATION,        /* conv type */
    AP_NONE,            /* sync level  */
    "",                 /* reserved    */
    AP_WHEN_SESSION_ALLOCATED,   /* return control */
    "",                 /* reserved    */
    "",                 /* partner lu alias    */
    "",                 /* mode name   */
    "",                 /* tp name     */
    AP_NONE,            /* security    */
    ""};                        /* reserved     */
alloc_rec.opext = (char)conv_type;
alloc_rec.conv_type = (char)conv_type;
memcpy(alloc_rec.tp_id, tp_id, sizeof(alloc_rec.tp_id));
memcpy(alloc_rec.plu_alias, partner_lu_name, sizeof(alloc_rec.plu_alias));
memcpy(alloc_rec.mode_name, mode_name, sizeof(alloc_rec.mode_name));
memset(alloc_rec.tp_name, 0x40, sizeof(alloc_rec.tp_name));
memcpy(alloc_rec.tp_name, tpn, tpn_len);
alloc_rec.rtn_ctl = (char)return_control;
alloc_rec.sync_level = (char)sync_level;
alloc_rec.security = (char)security;
if (security == AP_PGM) {
    memset(alloc_rec.pwd, 0x40, sizeof(alloc_rec.pwd));
    memcpy(alloc_rec.pwd, password, password_len);
    memset(alloc_rec.user_id, 0x40, sizeof(alloc_rec.user_id));
    memcpy(alloc_rec.user_id, user_id, user_id_len);
    }
APPC_C((long)(char far *)&alloc_rec);
*conv_id = alloc_rec.conv_id;
```

```
        *ret2 = alloc_rec.secondary_rc;
        return alloc_rec.primary_rc;
        }
        unsigned short
APPC_allocate(        char *    tp_id,
            char *    partner_lu_name,
            char *    mode_name,
            char *    tpn,            unsigned short    tpn_len,
            unsigned short    return_control,
            unsigned short    sync_level,
            unsigned short    security,
            char *    password,       unsigned short    password_len,
            char *    user_id,        unsigned short    user_id_len,
            long *    conv_id,
            long *    ret2)
{
        return allocate(AP_BASIC_CONVERSATION,
            tp_id,
            partner_lu_name,    mode_name,
            tpn,            tpn_len,
            return_control,
            sync_level,
            security,
            password,            password_len,
            user_id,            user_id_len,
            conv_id,
            ret2);
        }


unsigned short
APPC_MC_allocate(    char *    tp_id,
            char *    partner_lu_name,
            char *    mode_name,
            char *    tpn,
            unsigned short    tpn_len,
            unsigned short    return_control,
            unsigned short    sync_level,
            unsigned short    security,
            char *    password,
            unsigned short    password_len,
            char *    user_id,
            unsigned short    user_id_len,
            long *    conv_id,
```

```
        long *      ret2)
{

    return allocate(AP_MAPPED_CONVERSATION,
            tp_id,
            partner_lu_name,     mode_name,
            tpn,                 tpn_len,
            return_control,
            sync_level,
            security,
            password,            password_len,
            user_id,             user_id_len,
            conv_id,
            ret2);

}
```

B.3 CONFIRM.C

```
#include "appc_c.h"
#include <string.h>

static unsigned short
confirm(unsigned short    conv_type,
    char       *tp_id,
    long       conv_id,
    unsigned short       *rts,
    long       *ret2)
{
    static struct confirm confirm_rec = {
        AP_B_CONFIRM,              /* op code */
        AP_BASIC_CONVERSATION,         /*extended op code */
        0,                  /* reserved */
        0,                  /* return code */
        0L,                 /* secondary rc */
        "",                 /* TP_ID */
        0L,                 /* conversation id */
        };

    confirm_rec.opext = (unsigned char)conv_type;
    memcpy(confirm_rec.tp_id, tp_id, sizeof(confirm_rec.tp_id));
    confirm_rec.conv_id = conv_id;
    APPC_C((long)(char far *)&confirm_rec);
    *rts = confirm_rec.rts_rcvd;
    *ret2 = confirm_rec.secondary_rc;
    return confirm_rec.primary_rc;
    }

unsigned short
```

```
APPC_confirm(char    *tp_id,
    long        conv_id,
    unsigned short      *rts,
    long                *ret2)
{
    return confirm(AP_BASIC_CONVERSATION,
            tp_id,
            conv_id,
            rts,
            ret2);
    }


unsigned short
APPC_MC_confirm(char    *tp_id,
    long        conv_id,
    unsigned short      *rts,
    long        *ret2)
{
    return confirm(AP_MAPPED_CONVERSATION,
            tp_id,
            conv_id,
            rts,
            ret2);
    }
```

B.4 CONFIRMD.C

```
#include "appc_c.h"
#include <string.h>

static unsigned short
confirmed(unsigned short      conv_type,
    char        *tp_id,
    long        conv_id,
    long        *ret2)
{
    static struct confirmed confirmed_rec = {
        AP_M_CONFIRMED,            /* op code */
        AP_MAPPED_CONVERSATION,        /* extended op code */
        0,                  /* reserved */
        0,                  /* return code */
        0L,                 /* secondary rc */
        "",                 /* TP_ID */
        0L                  /* conversation id */
        };
    confirmed_rec.opext = (unsigned char)conv_type;
    memcpy(confirmed_rec.tp_id, tp_id, sizeof(confirmed_rec.tp_id));
    confirmed_rec.conv_id = conv_id;
    APPC_C((long)(char far *)&confirmed_rec);
```

```
     *ret2 = confirmed_rec.secondary_rc.;
     return confirmed_rec.primary_rc;
     }

unsigned short
APPC_MC_confirmed(char   *tp_id,
     long       conv_id,
     long       *ret2)
{
     return confirmed(AP_MAPPED_CONVERSATION,
             tp_id, conv_id, ret2);
     }

unsigned short
APPC_confirmed(char      *tp_id,
     long       conv_id,
     long       *ret2)
{
     return confirmed(AP_BASIC_CONVERSATION,
             tp_id, conv_id, ret2);
     }
```

B.5 DEALLOC.C

```
#include "appc-c.h"
#include "shalloc.h"
#include <stdlib.h>
#include <string.h>
#include <stddef.h>

static unsigned short
deallocate(unsigned short      conv_type,
     char       *tp_id,
     long       conv_id,
     unsigned short     type,
     unsigned short     log_data_len,
     char       *log_data,
     long       *ret2)
{
     static struct deallocate deallocate_rec = {
         AP_M_DEALLOCATE,          /* op code */
         AP_MAPPED_CONVERSATION,      /* extended op code */
         0,                  /* reserved */
         0,                  /* return code */
         0L,                 /* secondary rc */
         "",                 /* TP_ID */
         0L                  /* conversation id */
         };
```

```
      char far   *log_dptr;

      deallocate_rec.opext = (unsigned char)conv_type;
      memcpy(deallocate_rec.tp_id, tp_id, sizeof(deallocate_rec.tp_id));
      deallocate_rec.conv_id = conv_id;
      deallocate_rec.dealloc_type = (char)type;
      deallocate_rec.log_dlen = log_data_len;
      if (log_data_len > 0)
      {
            log_dptr = shalloc(log_data_len);
            fmemcpy(log_dptr, log_data, log_data_len);
            }
      else
            log_dptr = NULL;

      deallocate_rec.log_dptr = log_dptr;
      APPC_C((long)(char far *)&deallocate_rec);
      shfree(log_dptr);
      *ret2 = deallocate_rec.secondary_rc;
      return deallocate_rec.primary_rc;
      }

unsigned short
APPC_MC_deallocate(char *tp_id,
      long        conv_id,
      unsigned short      type,
      long        *ret2)
{
      return deallocate(AP_MAPPED_CONVERSATION,
                        tp_id,
                        conv_id,
                        type,
                        0,
                        NULL,
                        ret2);
      }
unsigned short
APPC_deallocate(char      *tp_id,
      long        conv_id,
      unsigned short      type,
      unsigned short      log_data_len,
      char        *log_data,
      long        *ret2)
{
      return deallocate(AP_BASIC_CONVERSATION,
                        tp_id,
                        conv_id,
                        type,
                        log_data_len,
                        log_data,
                        ret2);
}
```

B.6 RECALLOC.C

```c
#include "appc-c.h"
#include <stdlib.h>
#include <string.h>
unsigned short
APPC_receive_allocate(  char *              tp_name,
                        char *              tp_id,
                        long *              conv_id,
                        unsigned short*     sync_level,
                        unsigned short*     conversation_type,
                        char *              user_id,
                        char *              lu_alias,
                        char *              partner_lu_name,
                        char *              mode_name,
                        long *              ret2)
{
      static struct receive_allocate rec_alloc_rec = {
      AP_RECEIVE_ALLOCATE,          /* op code     */
      0,                /* reserved    */
      0,                /* return code     */
      0,                /* reserved    */
      OL,               /* secondary rc  */
      "",               /* tp name     */
      "",               /* TP_ID */
      OL,               /* conversation id  */
      AP_NONE,          /* sync level  */
      AP_BASIC_CONVERSATION,       /* conv type    */
      "",               /* user id     */
      "",               /* LU alias    */
      "",               /* partner lu alias      */
      ""                /* mode name   */
      };

      memcpy(rec_alloc_rec.tp_name, tp_name, 64);
      APPC_C((long)(char far *)&rec_alloc_rec);

      memcpy(tp_id, rec_alloc_rec.tp_id, sizeof(rec_alloc_rec.tp_id));
      *conv_id = rec_alloc_rec.conv_id;
      *sync_level = (unsigned short)rec_alloc_rec.sync_level;
      *conversation_type = (unsigned short)rec_alloc_rec.conv_type;
      memcpy(lu_alias, rec_alloc_rec.lu_alias, sizeof(rec_alloc_rec.lu_alias));
      memcpy(user_id, rec_alloc_rec.user_id, sizeof(rec_alloc_rec.user_id));
      memcpy(partner_lu_name, rec_alloc_rec.plu_alias,
                                      sizeof(rec_alloc_rec.plu_alias));

      memcpy(mode_name, rec_alloc_rec.mode_name, sizeof(rec_alloc_rec.mode_name));
      *ret2 = rec_alloc_rec.secondary_rc;
      return rec_alloc_rec.primary_rc;
}
```

B.7 RECVWAIT.C

```
=include "appc-c.h"
#include <string.h>
#include "shalloc.h"

static unsigned short
receive-and-wait(unsigned short    conv-type,
          char        *tp-id,
          long        conv-id,
          char        *data-ptr,
          unsigned short    max-length,
          unsigned short    *data-length,
          unsigned short    *what-received,
          unsigned short    *rts-received,
          long        *ret2)
{
     static struct receive-and-wait receive-and-wait-rec = {
          AP-B-RECEIVE-AND-WAIT,        /* op code */
          AP-MAPPED-CONVERSATION,       /* extended op code */
          0,                 /* reserved */
          0,                 /* return code */
          OL,                /* secondary rc */
          "",                /* TP-ID */
          OL                 /* conversation id */
          };

     char far  *dptr;

     receive-and-wait-rec.opext = (unsigned char)conv-type;
     memcpy(receive-and-wait-rec.tp-id, tp-id, sizeof(receive-and-wait-rec.tp-id));
     receive-and-wait-rec.conv-id = conv-id;
     dptr = shalloc(max-length);
     receive-and-wait-rec.dptr = dptr;
     receive-and-wait-rec.max-len = max-length;
     APPC-C((long)(char far *)&receive-and-wait-rec);

     *data-length = receive-and-wait-rec.dlen;
     fmemcpy(data-ptr, dptr, receive-and-wait-rec.dlen);
     shfree(dptr);
     *what-received = receive-and-wait-rec.what-rcvd;
     *rts-received = receive-and-wait-rec.rts-rcvd;
     *ret2 = receive-and-wait-rec.secondary-rc;
```

```
        return receive_and_wait_rec.primary_rc;
    }


unsigned short
APPC_MC_receive_and_wait(char        *tp_id,
        long        conv_id,
        char        *data_ptr,
        unsigned short        max_length,
        unsigned short        *data_length,
        unsigned short        *what_received,
        unsigned short        *rts_received,
        long        *ret2)
{
        return receive_and_wait(AP_MAPPED_CONVERSATION,
                        tp_id,
                        conv_id,
                        data_ptr,
                        max_length,
                        data_length,
                        what_received,
                        rts_received,
                        ret2);
    }


unsigned short
APPC_receive_and_wait(char        *tp_id,
        long        conv_id,
        char        *data_ptr,
        unsigned short        max_length,
        unsigned short        *data_length,
        unsigned short        *what_received,
        unsigned short        *rts_received,
        long        *ret2)
{
        return receive_and_wait(AP_BASIC_CONVERSATION,
                        tp_id,
                        conv_id,
                        data_ptr,
                        max_length,
                        data_length,
                        what_received,
                        rts_received,
                        ret2);
    }
```

B.8   SEND-ERR.C

```c
#include "appc-c.h"
#include "shalloc.h"
#include <string.h>
#include <stddef.h>

static unsigned short
send_error(unsigned short    conv_type,
           char         *tp_id,
           long         conv_id,
           unsigned short    type,
           unsigned short    log_data_length,
           char         *log_data_ptr,
           unsigned short    *rts_received,
           long         *ret2)
{
     static struct send_error send_error = {
          AP_M_SEND_ERROR,          /* op code */
          AP_MAPPED_CONVERSATION,        /* extended op code */
          0,                   /* reserved */
          0,                   /* return code */
          0L,                  /* secondary rc */
          "",                  /* TP_ID */
          0L                   /* conversation id */
          };

     char far  *log_dptr;

     send_error.opext = (unsigned char)conv_type;
     memcpy(send_error.tp_id, tp_id, sizeof(send_error.tp_id));
     send_error.conv_id = conv_id;
     send_error.err_type = (char)type;
     send_error.log_dlen = log_data_length;
     if (log_data_length > 0)
     {
          log_dptr = shalloc(log_data_length);
          fmemcpy(log_dptr, log_data_ptr, log_data_length);
     }
     else
          log_dptr = NULL;

     send_error.log_dptr = log_dptr;
     APPC_C((long)(char far *)&send_error);
     shfree(log_dptr);

     *rts_received = send_error.rts_rcvd;
     *ret2 = send_error.secondary_rc;
     return send_error.primary_rc;
     }
```

```c
unsigned short
APPC_MC_send_error(char *tp_id,
        long        conv_id,
        unsigned short      *rts_received,
        long      *ret2)
{
    return send_error(AP_MAPPED_CONVERSATION,
                        tp_id,
                        conv_id,
                        AP_PROG,
                        0,
                        NULL,
                        rts_received,
                        ret2);
}

unsigned short
APPC_send_error(char      *tp_id,
        long      conv_id,
        unsigned short      type,
        unsigned short      log_data_length,
        char      *log_data_ptr,
        unsigned short      *rts_received,
        long      *ret2)
{
    return send_error(AP_BASIC_CONVERSATION,
                        tp_id,
                        conv_id,
                        type,
                        log_data_length,
                        log_data_ptr,
                        rts_received,
                        ret2);
}
```

B.9   SENDDATA.C

```c
#include "appc_c.h"
#include "shalloc.h"
#include <string.h>

static unsigned short
send_data(unsigned short      conv_type,
        char      *tp_id,
        long      conv_id,
        unsigned short      data_length,
        char      *data_ptr,
        unsigned short      *rts_received,
        long      *ret2)
{
```

```
        static struct send_data send_data = {
            AP_B_SEND_DATA,                 /* op code */
            AP_MAPPED_CONVERSATION          /* extended op code */
            0,                  /* reserved */
            0,                  /* return code */
            OL,                 /* secondary rc */
            "",                 /* TP_ID */
            OL                  /* conversation id */
            };

        char far  *dptr;

        send_data.opext = (unsigned char)conv_type;
        memcpy(send_data.tp_id, tp_id, sizeof(send_data.tp_id));
        send_data.conv_id = conv_id;
        dptr = shalloc(data_length);
        fmemcpy(dptr, data_ptr, data_length);
        send_data.dlen = data_length;
        send_data.dptr = dptr;
        APPC_C((long)(char far *)&send_data);
        shfree(dptr);
        *rts_received = send_data.rts_rcvd;
        *ret2 = send_data.secondary_rc;
        return send_data.primary_rc;
        }

unsigned short
APPC_MC_send_data(char    *tp_id,
        long        conv_id,
        unsigned short      data_length,
        char        *data_ptr,
        unsigned short      *rts_received,
        long        *ret2)
{
        return send_data(AP_MAPPED_CONVERSATION,
                    tp_id,
                    conv_id,
                    data_length,
                    data_ptr,
                    rts_received,
                    ret2);
        }

unsigned short
APPC_send_data(char         *tp_id,
        long        conv_id,
        unsigned short      data_length,
        char        *data_ptr,
        unsigned short      *rts_received,
        long        *ret2)
{
```

```
        return send_data(AP_BASIC_CONVERSATION,
                         tp_id,
                         conv_id,
                         data_length,
                         data_ptr,
                         rts_received,
                         ret2);
}
```

B.10   TPSTART.C

```
#include "appc-c.h"
#include <string.h>

unsigned short
APPC_tp_started(char      *lu_id,
        char       *tp_name,
        unsigned short      tp_name_len,
        char       *tp_id)
{
    static struct tp_started tp_started_rec = {
        AP_TP_STARTED,
        0,
        };

    memset(tp_started_rec.lu_alias, ' ' , sizeof(tp_started_rec.lu_alias));
    memcpy(td_started_rec.lu_alias, lu_id, strlen(lu_id));
    memset(tp_started_rec.tp_name, 0x40, sizeof(tp_started_rec.tp_name));
    memcpy(tp_started_rec.tp_name, tp_name, tp_name_len);
    APPC_C((long)(char far *)&tp_started_rec);
    memcpy(tp_id, tp_started_rec.tp_id, sizeof(tp_started_rec.tp_id));
    return tp_started_rec.primary_rc;
    }
```

B.11   TPENDED.C

```
#include "appc-c.h"
#include <string.h>

unsigned short
APPC_TP_ended(char *tp_id)
{
```

```
    static struct tp-ended tp-ended-rec = {
        AP-TP-ENDED,
        AP-BASIC-CONVERSATION,
        };

    memcpy(tp-ended-rec.tp-id, tp-id, sizeof(tp-ended-rec.tp-id));
    APPC-C((long)(char far *)&tp-ended-rec);
    return tp-ended-rec.primary-rc;
    }
```

B.12 CONVERT.C

```
#include "acssvcc.h"
#include <stdlib.h>
#include <string.h>

short
convert(  unsigned short dir,
          unsigned short type,
          unsigned short len,
          char *         source,
          char *         target)
{
    static struct convert convert-rec =
    {
        SV-CONVERT};         /* Verb operation code */

    convert-rec.direction = (unsigned char)dir;
    convert-rec.char-set = (unsigned char)type;
    convert-rec.len = len;
    convert-rec.source = source;
    convert-rec.target = target;
    ACSSVC-C((long)(char far *)&convert-rec);
    return (short)convert-rec.primary-rc;
    }
```

B.13 SHALLOC.H

```
char far *shalloc(unsigned int);
void      shfree(char far *);
void      fmemcpy(char far *, char far *, unsigned int);
```

B.14   SHALLOC.C

```
/*    shalloc - a pair of functions (shalloc and shfree) like malloc and
 *    free, but which allocate and free within a shareable segment.
 *    Another function, fmemcpy, is like memcpy but copies to and from
 *    far pointers.
 */
#include <os2.h>
#include <stddef.h>
#include <memory.h>
/*    This union is for the grotesque macros for manipulating
 *    pointers on this brain-damaged 80286.
 */
static union   {
     struct {
          short    __off;
          short    __seg;
          } __x;
     char far  *__y;
     }__z;
#define offset(ptr) ((short)(char near *)(ptr))
#define segment(ptr)     (__z.__y = ((char far *)ptr), __z.__x.__seg)
#define address(seg, off) (__z.__x.__seg = seg,__z.__x.__off = off,__z.__y)
static unsigned int    seg = NULL;
static unsigned int    size;
#define    INITSIZE 1024
#define    INCSIZE   256
char far *
shalloc(len)
unsigned int        len;
{
     char far *adr;
     unsigned int  off;
     if (seg == NULL)
     {
          DosAllocSeg(INITSIZE, &seg, 3);
          DosSubSet(seg, 1, INITSIZE);
          size = INITSIZE;
          }
     len = (len+5) & ~3;
     while(DosSubAlloc(seg, &off, len) == 311)
     {
          size += INCSIZE;
          DosReallocSeg(size, seg);
          DosSubSet(seg, 0, size);
          }
     adr = address(seg, off);
     *(int far *)adr = len;
     return adr + 2;
     }
```

```
void
shfree(ptr)
char far  *ptr;
{
     unsigned int  len;
     if(ptr == NULL)
          return;
     ptr -= 2;
     len = *(int far *)ptr;
     DosSubFree(seg, offset(ptr), len);
     }
void
fmemcpy(dest, src, len)
char far *dest;
char far *src;
unsigned int  len;
{
     int seg;

     seg = segment(dest);
     movedata(segment(src), offset(src), seg, offset(dest), len);
     }
```

Index